Library of
Davidson College

Special Libraries
and Information Services
in India and in the U.S.A.

J. Saha

Chief Librarian
Indian Statistical Institute

The Scarecrow Press, Inc.
Metuchen, N.J.   1969

Copyright 1969 by J. Saha
SBN 8108-0257-0

Sponsored in part by the Air Force
Office of Scientific Research, Office
of Aerospace Research, under Grant
AF-AFOSR-531-66.

Contents

Part I - India

1. Organization of Science in India ... 5
2. Library Services in India ... 20
3. Bibliographical Services in India ... 28
4. Indian National Scientific Documentation Centre ... 50
5. Defence Scientific Information Centre ... 62
6. Indian National Bibliography ... 65
7. Documentation on Social Sciences ... 68
8. Education in Library Science and Documentation ... 79
9. Research in Library Science ... 95
10. Role of Library Associations ... 104

Part II - The U. S. A.

11. Prolegomena ... 111
12. Special Libraries and Technical Information Centers ... 126
13. Libraries and Machines ... 135
14. Library Education and Information Science ... 147
15. Trends in Research and Development ... 157

Appendix: Establishments Visited ... 168

021
S131a

70-1711

IN MEMORY OF

VIOLA SUSAN SHAW

Who was full of life
nd was interested in her friends
to the very end.

1. Organization of Science in India

Early History

In ancient India significant advances had been made in mathematics, astronomy, chemistry, medicine, and certain branches of biology. From about the third century B. C. close contacts with Greeks and from the eighth or ninth centuries A. D. with the Arabs, resulted in much exchange of scientific ideas and knowledge with the Middle East and Europe. The study of science and medicine continued to the end of the 12th century. This was followed by a period of general stagnation and scientific activities had practically ceased at the time of the rise of the European nations in the 17th and 18th centuries.

Nineteenth Century

With the growing influence of the British, the teaching of English started from about 1813 and at the initiative of some Indian leaders and Christian missionaries the Hindu College was established in Calcutta in 1817 as the first institution for teaching English, history, geography, mathematics, elementary science, etc. In 1837 English replaced Persian as the official language in law courts.

Back in 1784, however, the Asiatic Societ of Bengal was established in Calcutta by Sir William Jones who was a scholar and a judge of the Supreme Court. This society during the first century of its existence provided a house for meetings, a library, and a collection of ancient coins and medals as well as archaeological, technological and geological collections. The Journal of the Royal Asiatic Society of Bengal (started in 1832) was the first periodical in India for dissemination of the results of scientific work in the country. It published papers on zoology, botany and anthropometry with some papers on physics, meteorology, chemistry, geology and medical sciences and thus played a most important part in the advancement of science in India.

The Calcutta Botanical Garden was established in 1781 and the Botanical Survey of India was founded in Calcutta in 1889.

A school for surveying was established in Madras in 1793. The Trigonometrical Survey of the Peninsula of India was established in 1800, and in 1818 it was expanded as the Great Trigonometrical Survey. Topographical and Revenue Surveys were consolidated in 1817, and were amalgamated with the Trigonometrical Survey in 1878 to form the Survey of India. Since 1818 some geologists had been employed for survey work and the Geological Survey of India was founded in 1851.

Meteorological observatories and stations were set up in Madras in 1796, in Calcutta in 1824 and in Bombay in 1841; and a Meteorological Department for the whole of India was established in 1875.

An Agricultural Society was started in Calcutta in 1820. It became the Agricultural and Horticultural Society of India in 1823 and published its transactions and journals for a long time.

Elementary courses in engineering began to be provided in Bombay in 1824. The first engineering college was established in Roorkee in 1847. It has now been converted into an engineering university. Gradually, engineering colleges were established in Calcutta and at other places.

A Medical College was established in Calcutta in 1835. It provided training in physics, chemistry and botany as well as in anatomy and clinical subjects. A second Medical College was established, in Bombay, in 1845 with similar training facilities. Medical research was organized in 1869 and valuable work was done on clinical medicine and on the study of tropical diseases. There were early publications on medicine in the transactions of the Medical and Physical Society (1825-1845). A number of other medical journals were also published from time to time during the century.

Zoological and anthropometrical research had started in the Museum of the Asiatic Society in 1841 and was gradually strengthened with the foundation of the Indian Museum in 1856; these two sections were converted into the Zoological Survey of India in 1916 and

Science in India 7

the Anthropological Survey in 1946. The Archaeological Department came into existence in 1862. Three universities were established in Calcutta, Bombay, and Madras in 1857. The Universities of Punjab and Allahabad were established in 1882 and 1887, respectively. All five universities were of the examining and affiliating type, on the model of the London University and up to the beginning of the present century there was no provision for teaching in the universities themselves.

Early Twentieth Century

In the first half of the twentieth century there was some expansion in research facilities in the universities; and several research institutes in specialized fields were established both on private initiative and by the government. The private institutes made significant contributions in mathematical and physico-chemical subjects. In the government institutions the emphasis, up to the second world war, was on medicine and agriculture. Facilities for engineering and technological research, however, remained extremely meager; and research in biological subjects was not well developed until independence.

After almost fifty years of university education, the pattern began to change and provision for postgraduate teaching was made in Calcutta University in 1909. The foundation of the University College of Science in Calcutta in 1917 gave a great impetus to scientific research and it led to the establishment of research laboratories in other universities.

Government Institutions

The government concentrated on developing specialized institutes, especially in medicine and agriculture. The Haffkine Institute was established in Bombay in 1899, originally as a plague research laboratory. It gradually developed into an important center of research of preventive medicine. The Central Research Institute for Medical Research was started at Kasauli in 1906 and, in 1927, one of its sections developed into the Malaria Survey of India. The Nutrition Research Institute was established at Coonoor in 1928 and the All-India Institute of Public Health and Hygiene was set up in 1934.

Other medical institutes, such as King Institute of Preventive Medicine at Madras in 1903, Pasteur Institute at Coonoor in 1907, Medical Research Institute at Shillong in 1917 and the School of Tropical Medicine in Calcutta in 1921, were started by state governments. The Indian Research Fund Association, started in 1911 for the promotion of medical research, was later renamed the Indian Council of Medical Research (ICMR).

In the field of agriculture, the Agricultural Research Institute, founded at Pusa in 1903, was transferred to New Delhi in 1934. Next came the Forest Research Institute at Dehra Dun in 1906, the Tocklai Experimental Station, in 1911 in Assam, for research on tea, the Dairy Institute at Bangalore in 1920, the Cotton Technological Institute in Bombay in 1924, the Institute of Plant Industry at Indore in 1924, the Institute of Veterinary Research at Muktsar in 1925, the Lac Research Institute at Ranchi in 1925, the Institute of Sugar Technology at Kanpur in 1936 and the Jute Research Institute in Calcutta in 1939.

The Indian Council of Agricultural Research (ICAR) was established in 1929 with several associated committees for research in agricultural commodities (cotton, jute, sugar cane, oil seeds, tobacco, cocoanut, arecanut, etc.).

Hydrological research laboratories were established in Sind, the Punjab, and the United Provinces by the provincial governments in the 1930's; and the Central Water and Power Research Station at Poona by the central government in 1937.

To coordinate the scientific activities, the central government established the Board of Scientific Advice in 1902. This Board used to prepare annual reports on scientific progress. The activities of the Board were suspended in 1924.

Private Institutions

Several private research institutions came into existence during this period. The Indian Association for the Cultivation of Science, founded in 1876, became a most important center for physical research. The Bombay Natural History Society was founded in 1883. It published a long series of journals starting in 1886. The Indian Institute of Science was established in Bangalore in 1911, with generous financial support from J. N. Tata, and was developed as the first higher institute of engineering and technology. The Bose Institute was established in Calcutta by Jagadish Chandra Bose in 1917, with a wide program of biophysical research. The Indian Statistical Institute, established in Calcutta in 1931, is now the national center for research and training in both theoretical and applied statistics. The Indian Academy of Sciences founded by C. V. Raman at Bangalore in 1934 became a strong center for physical research. The Tata Institute of Fundamental Research, started in Bombay in 1945, is now closely associated with the Atomic Energy Commission. The Institute of Palaeobotany was established at Lucknow in 1946; the Physical Research Laboratory was established in Ahmedabad in 1948; the Institute of Radio Physics and Electronics was established in Calcutta in 1949; and the Institute of Nuclear Physics was started in Calcutta in 1951. About this time cancer research institutes were started in Calcutta and in Bombay. The Shri Ram Institute of Industrial Research was established in Delhi in 1947, being the first private institute of its kind. The Ahmedabad Textile Industry's Research Association was set up after independence as a joint endeavor of textile factories; several other associations were also formed on the same pattern. These research institutions, which were started on private initiative, began to make significant contributions to the progress of science.

Scientific Societies

A number of scientific societies, mainly for meetings and conferences, also began to be formed early in the twentieth century. Specialist societies had also been established much earlier but they were mostly of a local character. For example, the Mysore Institute of Engineers was established in 1863 and the Anthropological Society of Bombay in 1886, and both still continue to function as local institutions. There were other such societies which were active from time to time. The Mining and Geological Institute of India was founded in 1906 and it was followed by the Indian Mathematical Society in 1907; the Calcutta Mathematical Society in 1908; the Institution of Engineers, India in 1920; the Indian Botanical Society in 1921; the Indian Psychoanalytical Society in 1922; the Indian Chemical Society in 1924; the

Geological, Mining and Metallurgical Society of India in 1924; the Indian Psychological Association in 1925; the Society of Biological Chemists in 1931; the Indian Physical Society in 1934; the Bio-chemical Society in 1934; and the Indian Physiological Society in 1935 before the second world war. Since then several other societies such as the Zoological Society, the Entomological Society, the Institute of Chemists, the Indian Council of Ecological Research, and the Central Board of Geophysics, and several geographical societies have been established, some of which have active programs of research.

The earliest association of a general type covering many fields was the Asiatic Society of Bengal, founded in 1784. Some 130 years after the establishment of the Asiatic Society of Bengal, the Indian Science Congress Association came into existence in 1914 and has been, since that year, holding an annual congress of scientists in India. The United Provinces Academy of Sciences started in North India in 1930 was renamed the National Academy of Sciences in 1936. The Indian Academy of Sciences was established in 1934. The National Institute of Sciences was established in 1935, broadly on the model of the Royal Society of London but functioning in a somewhat different way. In addition to societies which had an all-India character, a number of regional societies arose in different parts of the country before the second world war.

Information on scientific societies and the role they have played in the promotion of science in the country is not readily available. The Survey and Planning of Scientific Research Unit of CSIR made an attempt, in 1963, to collect information on scientific societies in India. 115 societies of 150 such societies contacted replied to the questionnaires. A Directory of Science, Engineering and Technological Societies was compiled on the basis of the data collected. The cumulative growth of scientific societies is given in the following table.

It may be seen from this table that prior to 1940, there were only 38 societies and the societies began to be established at a much higher rate after independence. The figure almost doubled in ten years, and trebled by 1963.

Science in India

Cumulative Growth of Scientific Societies

Societies registered or established* up to the end of	Physical sciences	Medical sciences	Biological sciences	Engineering & Technological sciences	General	Total
1900	-	-	1	2	1	4
1910	1	3	1	3	2	10
1920	1	3	2	6	4	16
1930	3	4	5	10	5	27
1940	4	7	9	12	6	38
1950	11	15	15	20	10	71
1960	17	23	26	26	12	104
1963	18	26	26	26	14	110

* Information regarding the year of registration/establishment is not available for 5 societies, i.e., two in the biology group, two in the engineering group, and one in the general group.

Post-Independence Period

After independence in 1947 and particularly in the Second Five-Year Plan, which began in 1956, great emphasis was given to scientific research and industrialization. Factories for heavy machinery, heavy electrical equipment, machine tools, oil, chemicals and many light industries were being established.

There has also been a rapid increase in educational institutions of all types, especially from the period of the Second Five-Year Plan. Between 1857 and 1947, that is, in ninety years before independence, 19 universities were established. During the twenty years of independence, 43 new universities have been established and several higher educational institutions were empowered to award degrees. A list of the universities, giving the number of affiliated colleges, student enrolment and annual expenditure is provided at the end of this chapter (Appendix B). The University Grants Commission was established in 1956, on the British model, to guide the systematic progress of higher education.

Council of Scientific and Industrial Research (CSIR)

The Council of Scientific & Industrial Research was set up in 1942 as an autonomous body. The functions assigned to CSIR were all embracing in the matter of initiation, promotion and coordination of scientific and technological research in India.

The Council has now 39 research laboratories and institutes dealing with major disciplines in science or specializing in research bearing on major fields of industry. These include three industrial and technological museums, the Indian National Scientific Documentation Centre (INSDOC), Organisation for Medical Plants Cultivation, the Central Scientific Instruments Organisation, and the Indian Ocean Expedition. Some of the laboratories or institutes have field stations located in different parts of the country. A list of these laboratories with their year of establishment is given at the end of the chapter (Appendix A).

CSIR, with its chain of laboratories in various fields, is the largest organization for civilian research in India. It maintains close cooperation with the universities and institutes of higher technology and with the Indian Council of Agricultural Research, the Indian Council of Medical Research, the Atomic Energy Commission, the Railway Research and Designs Organization, the Defence Research and Development Organization, and with the Indian Standards Institution as well as with technical departments under different Ministries.

The CSIR laboratories communicate the results of research through presentation of research papers at symposia or seminars and through publication in research and technical journals. The Council publishes the following journals through its Directorate of Publications and Information:
1. Journal of Scientific & Industrial Research
2. Journal of Pure and Applied Physics
3. Indian Journal of Chemistry
4. Indian Journal of Technology
5. Indian Journal of Experimental Biology
6. Indian Journal of Biochemistry

Since 1959, CSIR has been publishing abstracts of published research papers from national research laboratories and a quarterly list of sponsored research projects, as a supplement to the Journal of Scientific and Industrial Research.

CSIR also publishes a science journal entitled Science Reporter, for dissemination of scientific information; a journal dealing with research pertaining to industry entitled Research & Industry; and a fortnightly bulletin named CSIR News. A standard encyclopaedia, the Dictionary of Indian Raw Materials and Industrial Products is in the process of publication under the popular title Wealth of India.

Growth of research activity under the Council has been rapid in recent years and a table showing the position in 1947, 1954, 1963 and 1966 is given below:

Year	Total number of Laboratories or Institutes	Budget (million R^S)	No. of Scientists or Technologists	Total No. of employees
1947-48	2	5.26	70	not available
1954-55	12	21.7	542	2993
1963-64	29	117.5	2435	11319
1966-67	39	163.6	8222*	15122

*This increase in number is due to redefinition of this cadre.

Expenditure by CSIR increased from $R^S 20$ millions in 1952-53 to $R^S 81$ millions in 1961-62. The rate of growth was 12.5 percent per annum from 1952-57 to 1957-58 and 21 percent per annum from 1957-58 to 1961-62. CSIR is now playing a very important role in the planning and formulation of science policy in India.

Besides the increased scientific research and development by the network of research laboratories under CSIR, normal activities of the scientific departments and institutes of government such as the Survey of India, the Geological Survey, the Zoological Survey of India, the Anthropological Survey of India, the Meteorological Department, the Indian Council of Medical Research, the Council of Agricultural Research, the Indian Forest Research Institute, the Indian Agricultural Research Institute, the Indian Veterinary Research Institute, the Central Water and Power Board, and various other institutes, departmental laboratories, and research units under the central and state governments expanded to several times their former level.

Government Expenditure on Research

In India, most of the research expenditure is incurred in government or quasi-government agencies and very little research funds are available from private sources. The universities and private scientific institutions have to depend mostly on government grants.

The steadily increased government expenditure on scientific research may give an idea of the growth and development of research activities in the country. The total expenditure on scientific research by the central and state governments during the period 1952-53 to 1961-62 is given in the table below:

Total Government Expenditure on Scientific Research
(in million rupees)

Year	Centers		States		Total	
	Current price level	1952-53 price level	Current price level	1952-53 price level	Current price level	1952-53 price level
1952-53	83.8	83.8	38.1	38.1	121.9	121.9
1955-56	153.6	166.1	35.8	38.7	189.4	204.8
1957-58	208.1	192.0	59.6	55.0	267.7	247.0
1958-59	233.5	206.9	80.6	71.4	314.1	278.3
1959-60	291.5	249.0	87.8	75.0	379.3	324.0
1960-61	313.7	251.4	98.9	79.2	412.6	330.6
1961-62	366.0	292.6	103.1	82.4	469.1	375.0

During this period, the expenditure increased from $R^S 122$ millions to $R^S 469$ millions. The rate of increase over the period 1952-53 to 1957-58 was 17 percent per annum; after 1957-58, however, it dropped 15 percent per annum.

The Centers' share of total government expenditure on research increased at a faster rate than that of the states. The amount increased from $R^S 84$ millions in 1952-53 to $R^S 366$ millions in 1962-63, while the expenditure by states increased only from $R^S 103$ millions. The Center had a 336 percent increase while the states recorded an increase of 171 percent.

The research expenditure incurred by the government has also been expressed on the basis of the 1952-53 price level. On this basis, the research expenditure was $R^S 247$ millions in 1957-58 and $R^S 375$ millions in 1961-62, an increase of 102 percent from 1952-53 to 1957-58 and 52 percent from 1957-58 to 1961-62. The rate of growth was, therefore, 15 percent per annum over the period of 1952-53 to 1957-58 and 11 percent per annum over the period 1957-58 to 1961-62.

Science in India 15

National Income & Expenditure on Research

The per capita expenditure on scientific research in India from 1952 to 1962 has been calculated on the basis that 90 percent of the expenditure on research has been increased by the government.

Per Capita Expenditure on Scientific Research and Proportion of Expenditure on Scientific Research to National Income in India

Year	population (millions)	total expenditure current price level (million R^S)	total expenditure 1952-53 price level (million R^S)	per capita expenditure current price level (R^S)	per capita expenditure 1952-53 price level (R^S)	national income of India at current price level (million R^S)	percentage of research expenditure to national income
1952-53	372	122.9	122.9	0.3277	0.3277	9,820	0.12
1955-56	387	189.4	204.8	0.4894	0.5292	9,980	0.19
1957-58	397	267.7	247.0	0.6743	0.6222	11,390	0.24
1959-60	425	379.3	324.0	0.8924	0.7624	12,940	0.29
1960-61	436	412.6	330.6	0.7583	0.7583	14,160	0.29
1961-62	440	469.1	375.0	1.0661	0.8523	14,630	0.32

Source: Journal of Scientific & Industrial Research, 22(12):484-85, 1963.

Although per capita expenditure on scientific research in India has shown a steady increase over the years, it is far from satisfactory when compared with more advanced countries. In the United States, the per capita expenditure on research was about 3.0 percent of per capita national income in 1961-62, while in India, it was only 0.3 percent.

Bibliographical References

Council of Scientific and Industrial Research Annual Report. New Delhi, 1966/67.

CSIR, Survey and Planning of Scientific Research Unit. Scientific Societies in India. New Delhi, 1965.

Indian Science Congress Association. Calcutta. Progress of Science in India during the Past Twenty-five Years. ed. by B. Prashad. 1938.

Mahalanobis, P. C. "Recent Developments in the Organization of Science in India" (Sankhya: The Indian Journal of Statistics, 25, series B, Pts. 1 & 2, p. 67-84, 1963).

Rahman, A. and others "A Study of Government Expenditure on Expenditure on Scientific Research" (Journal of Scientific and Industrial Research 22(12):479-86, 1963.

Report of the Reviewing Committee of the Council of Scientific and Industrial Research, 3rd report, New Delhi, 1964.

Syed, Nurullah and Naik, J. P. History of Education in India, ed. 2. Macmillan, 1951.

Appendix A
List of National Laboratories and Organizations under the CSIR giving the year of establishment

I. National Laboratories

1. National Chemical Laboratory (NCL), Poona, 1950
2. National Physical Laboratory (NPL), New Delhi, 1950
3. Central Fuel Research Institute (CFRI), Jealgora, 1950
4. Central Glass & Ceramic Research Institute (CGCRI), Calcutta, 1950
5. Central Food Technological Research Institute (CFTRI), Mysore, 1950
6. National Metallurgical Laboratory (NML), Jamshedpur, 1950
7. Central Drug Research Institute (CDRI), Lucknow, 1951
8. Central Road Research Institute (CRRI), New Delhi, 1952
9. Central Electro-Chemical Research Institute (CECRI), Karaikudi, 1953
10. Central Leather Research Institute (CLRI), Madras, 1953
11. Central Building Research Institute (CBRI), Roorkee, 1953
12. National Botanical Gardens (NBG), Lucknow, 1953
13. Central Electronics Engineering Research Institute (CEERI), Pilani, 1953
14. Central Salt and Marine Chemicals Research Institute (CSMCRI), Bhavnagar, 1954
15. Central Mining Research Station (CMRS), Dhanbad, 1955
16. Regional Research Laboratory (RRL), Hyderabad, 1956
17. Indian Institute for Experimental Medicine (IIEM), Calcutta, 1956
18. Regional Research Laboratory (RRL), Jammu, 1957
19. Central Mechanical Engineering Research Institute (CMERI), Durgapur, 1958
20. Central Indian Medicinal Plants Organization (CIMPO), Lucknow, 1959
21. Central Public Health Engineering Research Institute (CPHERI), Nagpur, 1959
22. Central Scientific Instruments Organization (CSIO), Chandigarh, 1959
23. National Aeronautical Laboratory (NAL), Bangalore, 1960
24. Indian Institute of Petroleum (IIP), Dehra Dun, 1960
25. National Geophysical Research Institute (NGRI), Hyderabad, 1961
26. Regional Research Laboratory (RRL), Jorhat, 1961
27. National Institute of Oceanography (NIO), New Delhi, 1962
28. Regional Research Laboratory (RRL), Bhubaneswar
29. Structural Engineering Research Centre (SERC), Roorkee

30. Industrial Toxicological Research Centre (ITRC), Lucknow

II. Industrial & Technological Museum

31. Birla Industrial & Technological Museum (BITM), Calcutta, 1959
32. Visvesvaraya Industrial & Technological Museum (VITM), Bangalore, 1962
33. Mafatlal Scientific & Technological Museum (MSTM), Bombay

III. Scientific & Technical Service Organization

34. Directorate of Scientific and Technical Personnel (DSTP), New Delhi, 1948
35. Publications and Information Directorate (PID), New Delhi, 1951
36. Indian National Scientific Documentation Centre (INSDOC), New Delhi, 1951
37. Directorate of Research Co-ordination, Industrial Liaison Unit (DRCIL), New Delhi, 1963
38. Central Design and Engineering Organization (CDEO), New Delhi, 1963
39. Survey and Planning of Scientific Research Unit (SPSRU), New Delhi, 1963

Appendix B

List of Universities in India giving the year of establishment and other information

Name and year of establishment	No. of colleges (1962-63)	No. of students (1962-63)	Expenditure (in R^S. crores) (1962-63)
(1)	(2)	(3)	(4)
1. Agra University, Agra (1927)	122	52,636	3.35
2. Agriculture University, Ludhiana (1962)			
3. Aligahr University, Aligarh (1921)	1	5,077	1.02
4. Allahabad University, Allahabad (1887)	6	8,892	0.94
5. Andhra University, Waltair (1926)	51	30,964	2.57
6. Andhra Pradesh Agricultural University, Hyderabad (1964)			
7. Annamalai University, Annamalainagar (1929)		3,164	0.62
8. Banaras Hindu University, Varanasi (1916)	19	7,634	3.07
9. Bangalore University, Bangalore (1964)			
10. Bhagalpur University, Bhagalpur (1960)	35	21,579	1.02
11. Bihar University, Muzaffarpur (1962)	38	29,854	1.62
12. Bombay University, Bombay (1857)	46	51,478	3.67
13. Burdwan University, Burdwan, West Bengal (1960)	69	21,782	1.58
14. Calcutta University, Calcutta (1857)	124	118,734	6.53

Appendix B (continued)

Name and year of establishment	No. of colleges (1962-63)	No. of students (1962-63)	Expenditure (in R^S. crores) (1962-63)
(1)	(2)	(3)	(4)
15. Delhi University, Delhi (1922)	29	23,081	4.27
16. Gauhati University, Gauhati (1948)	47	35,393	2.87
17. Gorakhpur University, Gorakhpur (1957)	28	14,814	0.80
18. Gujarat University, Ahmedabad (1949)	80	46,269	3.19
19. Indira Kala Sangeet Vishwavidyalaya, Khairagarh (1956)	29	149	0.01
20. Indore University, Indore (1964)			
21. Jabalpur University, Jabalpur (1957)	21	10,000	0.89
22. Jadavpur University, Jadavpur (1955)	3	3,808	0.71
23. Jammu and Kashmir University, Srinagar (1948)	32	10,540	1.14
24. Jawaharlal Nehru Krishi-Vishwa-Vidyalaya, Jabalpur (1964)			
25. Jiwaji University, Gwalior (1964)			
26. Jodhpur University, Jodhpur (1962)	1	4,530	0.35
27. Kalyani University, Kalyani, West Bengal (1960)	-	417	0.16
28. Kameshwara Singh Darbhanga Sanskrit University, Darbhanga (1961)	24	700	0.05
29. Karnatak University, Dharwar (1949)	39	16,961	1.83
30. Kerala University, Trivandrum (1937)	86	54,512	5.12
31. Kurukshetra University, Kurukshetra (1956)	3	797	0.36
32. Lucknow University, Lucknow (1921)	16	14,779	1.03
33. Madras University, Madras (1857)	117	61,995	6.79
34. Magadh University, Bodhgaya (1962)	30	22,444	0.75
35. M.S. University of Baroda, Baroda (1949)	15	10,247	1.25
36. Marathwada University, Aurangabad (1958)	23	8,118	0.99
37. Mysore University, Mysore (1916)	66	36,572	3.24
38. Nagpur University, Nagpur (1923)	58	31,022	2.54
39. North Bengal University, Siliguri (1962)	16	7,403	0.71
40. Orissa University of Agriculture and Technology, Bhubaneswar (1962)	2	972	0.23
41. Osmania University, Hyderabad (1918)	45	21,561	2.43
42. Punjab University, Chandigarh (1947)	138	57,268	5.68
43. Punjab University, Patiala (1962)	9	3,529	0.34
44. Patna University, Patna (1917)	10	11,212	1.24
45. Poona University, Poona (1949)	69	38,196	3.07
46. Rabindra Bharati, Calcutta (1962)		125	0.07
47. Rajasthan University, Jaipur (1947)	69	27,632	2.66
48. Ranchi University, Ranchi (1960)	26	19,980	2.10

49.	Ravi Shankar University, Raipur (1964)		
50.	Roorkee University, Roorkee (1949)	2,389	0.88
51.	Sardar Vallabhbhai Vidyapeeth, Vallabh Nagar, Anand (1955)	8	5,690	0.68
52.	Saugar University, Saugar (1946)	57	15,113	1.65
53.	Shivaji University, Kolhapur (1962)		
54.	S. N. D. T. Women's University, Bombay (1951)	13	4,030	0.30
55.	Shri Venkateswara University, Tirupati (1954)	15	10,415	1.32
56.	Udaipur University, Udaipur (1962)	3	1,019	0.31
57.	University of Agricultural Sciences, Bangalore (1964)		
58.	U. P. Agricultural University, Pantnagar, Nainital Distt. (1960)	3	667	0.58
59.	Utkal University, Cuttack (1943)	43	16,111	1.49
60.	Varanaseya Sanskrit Vishwavidyalaya, Varanasi (1958)		9,921	0.14
61.	Vikram University, Ujjain (1957)	58	27,242	2.54
62.	Visva Bharati University, Santiniketan (1951)	7	496	0.70

2. Library Services in India

In the previous chapter, I have given a brief account of the development of science and of the growth of academic and scientific institutions in India. As a corollary to the establishment of the institutions a number of libraries came into existence during the same period.

The third edition of the Indian Library Directory, issued by the Indian Library Association in 1951, and Libraries in India issued by the Government of India, Ministry of Education in 1952, have been the primary source of information about libraries in India up to the middle of this century. Both are outdated, but no attempt has yet been made to publish a comprehensive directory of the libraries in India. However, to give an idea of the origin and growth of libraries during the nineteenth century and the first half of the twentieth century, I have tabulated the information from these two source books.

Distribution of libraries by different categories and year of establishment

Year of establishment	Govt	Univ	Coll	Spec	Pub	Total	Cumulative Total
1781-1790					1	1	1
1791-1800							1
1801-1810					1	1	2
1811-1820			4		3	7	9
1821-1830			2		1	3	12
1831-1840			6		1	7	19
1841-1850			6	2	6	14	33
1851-1860	2	1	10	7	10	30	63
1861-1870	2		5	2	17	26	89
1871-1880	2	2	15	2	17	38	127
1881-1890	2		27	2	21	52	179
1891-1900	4		19	7	20	50	229
1901-1910	7	1	15	7	32	62	291
1911-1920	7	4	43	27	60	141	432
1921-1930	8	6	43	39	25	121	553
1931-1940	17	1	66	32	14	130	683
1941-1950	39	11	263	92	9	414	1097
date not known	26		19	5	9	60	1157
	116	26	543	225	247	1157	

The number of libraries in the country increased to 32 by 1850 and to 228 by 1900. By 1950 the number increased to 1157. Thus, 929 libraries were established during the first half of the twentieth century.

The first library in modern India was established in 1784, attached to the Asiatic Society of Bengal. That library now has a collection of about 150,000 volumes and receives about 500 periodicals. Next came the Library of the Asiatic Society of Bombay, originally known as the Bombay Literary Society, which was established in 1804. The present collection of this library, which is now the State Central Library of Bombay, is 427,466 volumes and 3,825 current periodicals. Through the inspiration of the Asiatic Society, two more societies with public libraries grew up at Calcutta during the next decade: the Delphian Society, in 1811, and the Calcutta Library Society, in 1818. Madras soon followed the lead of Bombay by establishing the Madras Literary Society in 1818, with a library open to the public. In 1830 another public library, the Bombay General Library, was founded in Bombay.

Calcutta Public Library, the forerunner of the Imperial Library, was established by the English community in Calcutta and was opened to the public in 1836. In 1860, management of the library was transferred to the Corporation of Calcutta, the municipal administration authorities. In 1901, the Imperial Library was established solely for the use of government officials. Lord Curzon, Viceroy of India, amalgamated the resources of the Calcutta Public Library with those of the Imperial Library in 1902 and opened the Imperial Library to the general public on January 30, 1903, with the following words: "It is intended that it should be a Library of reference, a working place for students, and a repository of materials for the future historians of India, in which as far as possible every work written about India at any time can be seen and read." With these objectives the Imperial Library developed and continued; after independence, in 1948, the name was changed to the National Library. The National Library's book collection, while it cannot quantitatively compare with the leading national libraries of the Western countries, is nevertheless rich in content. The library's stock of books is nearly 1.5 million and it receives over 9,000 current periodicals. It is the biggest library in India. The major part of the collection, however, is in the humanities and social sciences.

Another public library worth mentioning is the Connemara Public Library which was established in Madras in 1896. This library now functions as the State Central Library of Madras; it has a stock of 177,295 volumes and receives 5,068 current periodicals.

Under the Delivery of Books (Public Libraries) Act, 1954, amended in 1956, one copy of each book and other documents printed in India is to be sent to the National Library in Calcutta, the State Central Library (Connemara Public Library) in Madras, the State Central Library (Asiatic Society) in Bombay and to the Central Reference Library to be established in Delhi.

Calcutta, Bombay and Madras have the oldest university libraries in India and the Calcutta University Library has the richest collection. The resources of some of the bigger university libraries are given in the table below:

	University	Volumes	Periodicals
1.	Allahabad	218,266	834
2.	Banaras	363,382	3,306
3.	Baroda	212,586	1,429
4.	Bombay	275,000	1,186
5.	Calcutta	400,000	1,200
6.	Delhi	269,274	3,478
7.	Madras	248,516	2,032
8.	Punjab	222,575	1,450
9.	Visva Bharati	240,000	850

Laurence J. Kipp, in his report, Indian Libraries and the Indian Wheat Loan Educational Exchange Programme, (1961) recorded the size of the collections of 30 libraries surveyed.

Eight libraries had less than 50,000 volumes; 9 libraries had more than 50,000 but less than 100,000 volumes; 3 libraries, more than 100,000 but less than 150,000 volumes and 10 libraries had more than 150,000 volumes.

Most of the university libraries in India are not research libraries in the true sense because the emphasis in the universities so far has mainly been on teaching, not research. Dr. Carl M. White's recent fact finding survey of the present state of the University of Delhi Library and his recommendations would be helpful to set up the norm for the future development of university libraries in India.

Data from two other sources measure the growth of specialized libraries to 1960. In connection with the project of the Union Catalog of Periodicals, INSDOC in 1960 compiled a list of scientific libraries in the country. T. S. Rajagopalan in a paper, "National Grid of Scientific Libraries, " presented the data in the table reproduced below:

Period	1900 and before	1901 to 1910	1911 to 1920	1921 to 1930	1931 to 1940	1940 to 1950	1951 to 1955	1956 to 1960
Number of Libraries	35	20	35	39	35	80	75	96
Cumulated Total	35	55	90	129	164	244	319	415

The percentage of scientific libraries existing before the present century is only 9% and about 50% of the libraries have been established since independence. The table shows that 23% of the libraries were established during the five year period, 1955 to 1960.

In 1962, the Indian Association of Special Libraries and Information Centres attempted to compile a comprehensive directory of research and special libraries in India and sent a detailed questionnaire to about 500 libraries. It is unfortunate that only 173 libraries responded in spite of repeated reminders. Detailed information about historical background, stock, specialization and subjects covered, services offered, nature of clientele, expenditure, staff, etc. , about those 173 libraries has been presented in this directory. The directory also provided the names and addresses of about 850 libraries having special collections in science and technology, the social sciences and the humanities. Though the directory suffered from lack of comprehensiveness in coverage, it serves as a helpful reference to Indian librarians.

The resources in these libraries, however, developed very slowly. It may be pointed out at this stage that since English replaced

Persian as the official language in India in 1837, it gradually became the medium for instruction and communication at higher education and research levels. The literature produced in Western countries, particularly in England, formed the major part of the basic collection of the reading material. Due to lack of adequate funds, the library collection remained very incomplete and due to lack of trained and experienced personnel higher levels of readers' aid and bibliographical services were unknown except in very few libraries. The impact of scientific research and industrial research was negligible. The industries depended mostly on Western countries for information and technical know-how. The scientists, particularly those working in the fields of pure science, depended mostly on their own information sources. There was no social pressure for the emergence of documentation as a link in the communication chain. The libraries functioned simply as storehouses to serve the readers with books and periodicals on demand.

It is only since independence that there has been a steady expansion of research activities of the scientific departments, departmental laboratories, institutions, and organizations under the central and state governments. As a result of the three five-year plans and the government's policy on scientific and industrial research many new academic, research, and industrial organizations have been developed.

The demand for improved library facilities is an essential corollary to these new developments and to rapid drive for industrialization. To meet this new situation a number of special libraries in different fields of knowledge have come into existence, in addition to the older libraries which have been reorganized.

Since the inception of the University Grants Commission in 1953 the Commission has given serious thought to improving the resources of libraries attached to universities and other institutions of higher learning. The Commission is also attempting to standardize operation and to improve library services. With generous grants from the University Grants Commission a number of university libraries now have modern library buildings and improved book collections.

Library Services in India

In Indian libraries, particularly in those attached to scientific institutions and institutions of higher learning and research, about 75 to 80% of the book budget is spent on acquiring books, journals, and other reading materials from abroad because Indian students and researchers are mostly dependent on foreign literature, particularly in English, for their studies. This brings about the serious problem of time lag in the flow of materials as well as in the current bibliographic information reaching Indian libraries. Normally it takes about three months to receive literature by sea mail. The only satisfactory solution to this problem is to get all current periodicals and documents of research value by air mail, but this would be frightfully expensive. As a half-way solution to this problem it was felt that some arrangement should be made to reduce the time-gap about information on current research papers published in scientific and technical periodicals. INSDOC, immediately after its establishment in 1952, looked into this problem and decided to issue a documentation list to keep scientists and technologists informed about the current scientific literature published in periodicals. To reduce the time gap, INSDOC made arrangements with several foreign documentation centers and libraries to receive the content pages of important scientific periodicals by air mail immediately on publication. The first issue of the INSDOC List covering current scientific literature in all branches of science and technology appeared in 1954. The List, though very selective and covering only a very small percentage of the current periodicals literature, was well received by scientists and librarians as a documentation list for current awareness on different fields of science. The INSDOC List demonstrated the value of documentation activities and several special libraries gradually began to organize local documentation services specially designed and adapted for local users.

Unlike the U.K., the U.S.A., and several other Western countries, in India the special library, in the modern sense, has preceded the development of the public library. Except for some of the earlier libraries, which have grown in size over the years, most of the special libraries are small but they all attempt to operate on modern lines, using the techniques developed in the U.S.A. and in the

U. K. Most libraries use either the Dewey or the Universal Decimal Classification scheme. Only a few libraries have so far adopted Colon Classification for books and other literature. Two catalogs, in separate sequence--a classified catalog for subject and an author-title dictionary catalog--are generally maintained rather than a dictionary catalog as practiced in the U. S. A.

Most of these libraries now have up-to-date reference collections and selected international abstracting and indexing periodicals to provide reference and bibliographical services on demand. A limited number of libraries have staff translators for handling foreign languages and a small reprographic unit for microfilming or photoduplication work.

It is often difficult to find a really competent staff with a good academic background to manage the library. Some of the librarians attached to the special libraries issue local documentation lists to provide information to the scientists and researchers attached to those institutions either for current awareness or for retrospective searches. The processes and techniques for preparation of these documentation lists are more or less similar to the method used by the U. S. Department of Agriculture Library in preparation of the Bibliography of Agriculture in the 1950's. A more detailed account of the bibliographical services provided by the special libraries is given in a subsequent chapter. A list of some of the important libraries with their resources is given below.

sl. no.	Institution	Vols.	Periodicals
1	Geological Survey of India (1851)	190,000	850
2	Indian Agricultural Research Institute (1905)	140,000	1,200
3	Gokhale Institute of Politics and Economics (1905)	105,778	850
4	Forest Research Institute (1906)	80,000	600
5	Indian Institute of Science (1909)	61,000	1,000
6	Directorate General of Health Services Library (1926)	75,000	800
7	Indian Statistical Institute (1931)	115,000	2,300
8	Central Water and Power Commission Library and Information Bureau (1931)	54,000	300
9	Indian Council of World Affairs (1943)	97,000	1,500
10	Defense Science Organization Library (1949)	80,000	700

Bibliographical References

Indian Library Association Indian Library Directory, ed. 3, 1951.

India, Education (Ministry of) Libraries in India. 1951, 1952 (Publication 123).

Indian Association of Special Libraries and Information Centres Directory of Special and Research Libraries in India, 1964.

Rajagopalan, T. S. and Islam, S. I. "National Grid of Scientific Libraries." (Documentation and its Facets, edited by S. R. Ranganathan, 1963, p. 166-175.)

White, Carl M. A Survey of the University of Delhi Library. Delhi University Library, 1965.

3. Bibliographical Services in India

The scientists and technologists in India, though largely dependent on scientific literature and technological reports generated in Western countries, felt from the very beginning the need of some bibliographical control of Indian science literature. Scientists themselves undertook the responsibility in the absence of competent librarians and some have compiled well documented retrospective bibliographies on specific subjects. Given below is a selection of earlier bibliographies compiled by the scientists and scientific workers.

Earlier Bibliographies

1. Professional Papers on Indian Engineering. Classified list of papers. vols. 1-7, Roorkee, 1863-70.

2. Oldham, R. D. Bibliography of Indian Geology, being a list of books and papers published prior to 1887. Geological Survey of India, Calcutta, 1888, p. 145.

3. Sinclair, W. F. "Some New Books on Indian Zoology." Jour. Bombay Nat. Hist. Soc. 5:176-184, 1890.

4. Oryza, Sativa "Literature on the Races in India." Agriculture Ledger 16:1-594, 1910.

5. Blatter, E. "Bibliography of the Botany of British India and Ceylon." Jour. Bombay Nat. Hist. Soc. 20:79-176, 1911.

6. Imperial Department of Agriculture in India dealing with cotton 1906-1926. Indian Central Cotton Committee Bulletin No. 8, Bombay, 1927.

7. Sohoni, V. V. "Bibliography of Meteorological Papers in the Publications of the Asiatic Society of Bengal, 1788-1928." Jour. Proc. Asiatic Soc. Bengal, p. 454-502, 1929.

8. Shaw, F. J. R. & Bose, R. D. "List of Publications on the Botany of Indian Crops." Imperial Agricultural Research Institute, Pusa, Bull. No. 202, 1930.

9. Sinton, J. A. "Bibliography of Malaria in India." Records Malaria Survey of India, No. 1, 1930.

10. Butler, E. J. & Bisby G. R. Fungi of India, "Appendix V, Biblio-

graphy." Imperial Council of Agricultural Research Science Monograph No. 1, 1931.

11. Guha Roy, K. K. & Mahalanobis, P. C. Statistical Methods and Their Applications to Agronomy: a bibliography. Imperial Council of Agricultural Research, Misc. Bulletin No. 9, 1936, p. 126.

12. India. Industrial Research Bureau "Bibliography of Industrial Publications Published in India from 1921." Bulletin of Indian Industrial Research Bureau, 1936.

Abstracting Periodicals

The earliest attempt at an abstracting service for scientific literature was a monthly abstract of the medical sciences which was started in 1880. It was known as the Calcutta Medical News and was issued under the patronage of Surgeon Major D. B. Smith, Principal, Medical College, Bengal, and Surgeon Major J. M. Coates, Sanitary Commissioner, Bengal. It abstracted English periodicals and some French and German periodicals, as well as relevant quotations from Indian medical books in Sanskrit.

The first systematic attempt to provide a comprehensive abstracting service for Indian scientific literature was made by the National Institute of Sciences of India in 1935. The first volume of Indian Science Abstracts issued in 1936, contained an annotated bibliography of scientific articles published in India. Later volumes included abstracts of papers by Indian authors in foreign scientific periodicals. Roughly 2,000 articles were covered each year from 1935 through 1938. In 1939, publication ceased due to the outbreak of World War II and to lack of financial support.

In 1936, the Central Board of Irrigation started its abstracting periodical under the title Quarterly Bulletin. The Central Water and Power Commission continues this publication as Irrigation Abstracts. About 2,500 abstracts prepared by engineers and specialists are published annually.

The other pioneering abstracting periodicals in India are:
1. Journal of Medicine. An international medical abstracts and reviews journal. 1946 -, Bi-monthly. Calcutta.
2. Plant Protection Abstracts. Quarterly. Directorate of Plant Protection, New Delhi.

3. <u>Indian Horticulture</u>, incorporating Indian horticultural abstracts. Bi-monthly. Indian Council of Agricultural Research, New Delhi.

Systematic documentation in the field of forestry was organized in the Forest Research Institute, Dehra Dun. Articles published in scientific periodicals on forestry and its allied subjects were regularly scanned and indexed by the research workers in each department. A scheme of classification for forestry was developed in this Institute, which later formed the basis for the Oxford system of classification for forestry.

The scientific organizations with the help of scientific workers continued to publish ad hoc bibliographies outside the library, as most of the libraries continued functioning in a traditional way. The Madras University Library under the leadership of Dr. S. R. Ranganathan may claim to be the first library to provide "readers' aid" and bibliographic service to the research workers. Dr. Ranganathan, as far back as in 1928, began to provide subject bibliographies and reading lists to researchers on demand. On the basis of almost ten years' experience of such extended bibliographic service he wrote the book <u>Reference Service</u> in 1940. This book gave a new insight about library service to Indian librarians.

However, the general pattern of library service remained unchanged for many more years. For current scientific literature and information, scientists had to be satisfied by reading the periodicals received in the library and other literature that they could locate themselves. The international abstracting and indexing periodicals reach India several months after publication. Naturally those serve the Indian readers only for retrospective searches. This situation continued until the issuance of the <u>INSDOC List of Current Scientific Literature</u> by the Indian National Scientific Documentation Centre (INSDOC) in 1954. This may claim to be the first systematic documentation list issued in India with a view to keeping the scientists and scientific workers informed about current scientific literature on different subjects.

Local Documentation Lists

The establishment of the National Documentation Centre in 1952 and the issuance of the current documentation list from 1954 opened a new horizon to Indian scientists as well as to librarians. Until that time, scientists felt frustrated with traditional library services and pressed for improved services by well-trained librarians with subject backgrounds. Librarians also began to realize the importance of documentation work and services to meet the needs of specialists. Some of the special libraries having national status, or otherwise having a big collection of material in some subject field, started issuing abstracting or indexing periodicals or local documentation lists, in some form, for communication of current literature, particularly to scientists or researchers attached to their institutions. The usefulness of such a local list always crosses the boundary of that particular organization when it covers a large number of current periodicals and research reports, especially if the list is systematically indexed and is issued promptly.

In designing bibliographical services intelligently, there is need for a great deal of detailed information on the needs of users in all fields and the demand they make or could make on these services. From that point of view it is more reasonable to entrust the subject indexes to special libraries.

Special Librarians have built up a good record of the activity which is now described as documentation, i.e., cataloging, classification, indexing, abstracting, editing, translating and preparation of the materials of research value for publication. In a successful special library one can see high level amalgamation of technical services and readers' services.

It is obvious that the activities in many scientific laboratories and industrial research institutions are interdisciplinary. In order to minimize unnecessary duplication of resources, the libraries within a subject group are attempting to evolve some definite methods for coordinating and developing their resources and information service by forming library systems and networks of library systems.

A recent survey of the indexing and abstracting services in India by Mohan Bhatia of the Survey and Planning of Scientific Research Unit, CSIR, recorded that at present more than 60 indexing and abstracting periodicals for current awareness are issued by the special libraries and documentation centers in India. The compilers all attempt to make the lists exhaustive. A large percentage of these lists are issued in mimeographed form, and they are generally known as local documentation lists. It is unfortunate that though some of these lists are valuable for their design and coverage, very little attention has been given to standardization and coordination of these lists for bibliographical control and for development of coordinated service throughout India.

The classified list of these indexing and abstracting periodicals given below may give an idea of the activities, at the level of special institutions, to command the flow of scientific information in the country.

001.89   Research & Development

1. <u>CSIR Abstracts.</u> 1959-

Abstracts of research communications of the National Research Laboratories and sponsored research projects of CSIR are published in classified sequence in the Quarterly Supplement to the Journal of Scientific and Industrial Research.

2. <u>Index to Current R & D Literature.</u> 1965-

Survey & Planning of Scientific Research Unit, CSIR, New Delhi. Monthly. Mimeographed. Classified under subject headings.

3. <u>R & D Abstracts.</u> 1965-

Survey & Planning of Scientific Research Unit, CSIR, New Delhi. Quarterly. Mimeographed. Classified under subject headings.

5/6   Science & Technology in General

4. <u>Classified Documentation List of Current Scientific Literature,</u> 1964-

Central Salt & Marine Chemicals Research Institute, Bhavnagar. Monthly. Mimeographed. Classified under U.D.C.

5. <u>Desidoc List - Current Scientific Literature.</u> 1964-

Scientific Information Bureau. Defence Science Organization,

Bibliographical Services in India

New Delhi. Fortnightly. Printed. Classified under U. D. C. Index to the subject headings is given at the end.

6. Index to literature on science of science. 1966-

   Reseach Survey and Planning Organisation, CSIR, New Delhi. Monthly.

7. Indian Science Abstracts. 1965-

   Indian National Scientific Documentation Centre, New Delhi. Monthly. Printed. Classified under U. D. C. Author and key word indices are given at the end.

8. Library Bulletin. 1962-

   Central Food & Technological Research Institute, Mysore. Monthly. Mimeographed. Classified under Colon Classification.

9. Selected Scientific Literature. 1962-

   Planning & Information Section, Defence Research & Development Organisation, Defence Research Laboratory (Stores), Kanpur. Fortnightly. Mimeographed. Classified under subject headings.

10. Weekly Library Bulletin of Periodical Articles (Formerly Weekly Documentation Bulletin). 1964-

    Indian Institute for Biochemistry and Experimental Medicine, Calcutta. Weekly. Mimeographed. Title service under respective periodicals.

11. Weekly Title Service (LRDE).

    Technical Information Centre. Electronics & Radar Development Establishment, Bangalore. Weekly. Mimeographed. Title service under respective periodicals.

519. 2 Statistical Mathematics

12. Index to Statistical Literature. 1960-

    Index to Statistical Institute Library, Calcutta. Fortnightly. Mimeographed. Classified under subject headings.

55   Geology

13. Library Bulletin, Geological Survey of India. Section B. 1952-

    Geological Survey of India. Central Library, Calcutta. Fortnightly.

14. Bulletin of Current References on Petroleum & Geological Sciences. 1963-

Oil & Natural Gas Commission. Dehra-Dun. Quarterly.

57 Anthropology
 15. Documentation of Indian Anthropology.
   Anthropological Survey of India Library, Calcutta. Yearly. Mimeographed. Classified under subject headings. Subject index is given at the end.

59 Zoology
 16. Bibliography of Indian Zoology (with a Short Review). 1962-
   Zoological Survey of India, Calcutta. Annual. Mimeographed. Alphabetically by author.

61 Medical Sciences
 17. Index to Indian Medical Periodicals. 1954-
   Directorate General of Health Services Library, New Delhi. Half-yearly. Printed Classified.
 18. Medical Review of Reviews. 1939-
   12/1193 Shora Kothi, Subzimandi, Delhi. Monthly. Printed.

612 Physiology
 19. Documentation List: Current technical literature. 1965-
   Defence Institute of Physiology & Allied Sciences. Madras. Monthly.

615 Pharmacy, Pharmacology and Therapeutics
 20. Classified List of Current Scientific Literature. 1962-
   Documentation Unit, Central Drug Research Institute, Lucknow. Half-yearly. Mimeographed. Classified under subject headings.

621 Mechanical Engineering
 21. Bibliography on numerical control of machine tools. 1962-
   Hindusthan Machine Tools Ltd. Bangalore. Monthly.
 22. Current Technical Information. 1964-
   Hindusthan Machine Tools Ltd. Bangalore. Monthly.
 23. Contents List: Current engineering literature at CMERI. 1965-
   Central Mechanical Engineering Research Institute. Durgapur. Fortnightly.

621, 039:539.1   Nuclear Technology
24. Bibliography of Current Reports.
Information Division, Atomic Energy Establishment, Trombay. Mimeographed. Classified under subject headings. Index to report Nos. given at the end.
25. Microforms Bulletin. 1963-
Classification Section, Information Division, Atomic Energy Establishment, Trombay. Monthly. Mimeographed. Report nos. are mentioned thus making it a guide to research reports on the subject.

621.3   Electrical Engineering
26. Library Information Digest. 1963-
Heavy Electricals Ltd. Research & Development Division. Bhopal. Monthly.
27. Technical Information Bulletin. 1966-
Bharat Heavy Electricals Ltd. Central Designs. Tiruchirapalli. Monthly.

621.35:541.13   Electrochemistry
28. Programme and Abstracts of Papers...
Seminar of Electrochemistry. 1960-
Central Electrochemical Research Institute, Karaikudi. Annual. Printed. Respective section of the seminar. Author index is given at the end.

621.38   Electronics
29. CEERI Documentation List. 1965-
Central Electronics and Engineering Research Institute. Pilani. Monthly. Mimeographed. Classified under U. D. C.
30. DLRL Documentation List with Indicative Abstracts. 1965-
Defence Electronics Research Laboratory, Defence Research and Development Organisation. Hyderabad. Weekly.
31. LRDE Documentation List.
Technical Information Centre, Electronics & Radar Development Establishment (Defence), Bangalore. Fortnightly. Mimeographed. Classified under U. D. C.

622 Mining and Mineral Dressing
32. Index to Selective Articles. 1960-
Central Library, Indian Bureau of Mines, Nagpur. Monthly. Mimeographed. Classified under subject headings.

624 Civil Engineering
33. Civil Engineering Periodicals Index. 1964-
69 Kaka Nagar, New Delhi. Monthly (except in July). Printed. Classified under subject headings.

625.1/6 Railway Engineering
34. Documentation Notes. 1954-
Research Designs & Standards Organization, Ministry of Railways, Lucknow. Quarterly. Printed. Classified under U. D. C.

625.7 Highway Road Engineering
35. Articles in Current Periodicals.
Central Road Research Institute Library, New Delhi. Fortnightly. Mimeographed.
36. CRRI Road Abstracts. 1961-
Central Road Research Institute Library, New Delhi. Half-yearly. Printed. Classified under subject headings.
37. Highway Documentation. Recent Literature on Highway Engineering with Selected Abstracts & Annotations. 1965-
Central Road Research Institute Library, New Delhi. Mimeographed. Classified under U. D. C. and Colon Classification.

626.8:627.8 Irrigation, Drainage & Power
38. Bibliography of Irrigation, Drainage, River Training & Flood Control. 1956-
International Commission on Irrigation and Drainage, New Delhi. Half-yearly. Printed. Classified.
39. Abstracts (of Current Technical Literature) 1936-
Central Board of Irrigation & Power, New Delhi. Monthly. Printed. Classified under U. D. C.

629.13   Aeronautical Engineering
40. NALSDOC List: Current scientific literature. 1966-
    National Aeronautical Laboratory. Bangalore. Monthly.

63   Agriculture
41. Bibliography of Agriculture in India from Periodicals Received in the I.A.R.I. Library.
    Indian Agricultural Research Institute Library, New Delhi. Monthly. Mimeographed. Classified under subject headings.
42. Documentation of Agriculture - The Bulletin of Current References on Agriculture in India. 1959-
    Indian Council of Agricultural Research Library, New Delhi. Quarterly. Mimeographed. Classified under Colon Classification. Cumulative index to subject headings is given in the last issue of each year.

63:31   Agricultural Statistics
43. Statistical Newsletter and Abstracts. A Quarterly Journal of Abstracts of Statistical Papers and the Activities of the Institute of Agricultural Research Statistics. 1963-
    Indian Council of Agricultural Research. Quarterly. Printed. Alphabetically by author.

631.8   Fertilisers. Manuring
44. F.A.I. Abstract Service. 1962-
    Fertiliser Association of India, New Delhi. Monthly. Mimeographed. Classified under subject headings.

636/639   Animal Husbandry
45. Documentation of Animal Husbandry. The Bulletin of Current References on Animal Husbandry. 1959-
    Indian Council of Agricultural Research, New Delhi. Half-yearly. Mimeographed. Classified under colon classification. Cumulative index to subject headings is given in the last issue of each year.

639.2   Fisheries
46. Bibliography of Indian Fisheries. (Formerly Quarterly Bibli-

ography of Current Indian References on Fisheries and Allied Subjects).

  Central Inland Fisheries Research Institute, Calcutta. Quarterly. Mimeographed. Classified under U. D. C.

664   Food Industries
  47. Documentation list for food technology. 1966-
    CFTRI, Mysore. Monthly.
  48. Food Science & Technology Abstracts. 1966-
    Central Food Technological Research Institute, Mysore. Monthly.

666.12   Glass & Ceramics
  49. CGCRI Documentation List. 1966-
    Central Glass & Ceramic Research Institute, Calcutta. Monthly.

669.1   Iron and Steel
  50. Technical Bulletin.
    Tata Iron & Steel Co. Ltd. Information Department. Jamshedpur. Monthly.
  51. Advance Documentation List. 1965-
    Bhilai Steel Plant. Research and Control Laboratory, Bhilai. Monthly.

669.71   Aluminium Technology
  52. Alind Abstracts. 1950-
    The Aluminium Industries Limited, Kundara, Kerala. Bi-monthly. Printed. Classified under subject headings.

675   Leather Industry
  53. Current Leather Literature. 1967-
    Central Leather Research Institute, Madras. Monthly.
  54. Leather Titles Service. 1967-
    Central Leather Research Institute, Madras. (Irregular)

676.1   Paper & Pulp Technology
  55. Technical Abstracts. 1952-

Bibliographical Services in India   39

Cellulose and Paper Branch, Forest Research Institute and College, Dehra Dun. Half-yearly. Mimeographed. Classified under subject headings.

677   Textile
  56. BTRA Abstracts. 1958-

Bombay Textile Research Association, Bombay. Quarterly. Mimeographed. Classified under subject headings. Cumulative index is given in the last issue of each year.

  57. Current Textile Literature Classified Contents Lists with Abstracts. 1961-

Ahmedabad Textile Industries Research Association, Ahmedabad. Monthly. Mimeographed. Classified under subject headings.

676.46   Artificial Fibres
  58. Current Literature Bulletin. 1960-

National Rayons Corporation, Kalyan. Monthly. Mimeographed. Classified under subject headings.

69   Building Industry
  59. CBRI Abstracts. 1964-

Central Building Research Institute Library, Roorkee. Quarterly. Mimeographed. Classified under subject headings.

  60. CBRI Documentation List. 1965-

Central Building Research Institute, Roorkee. Weekly.

  61. N. B. O. Abstracts. 1956-

National Buildings Organisation, New Delhi. Monthly. Mimeographed. Classified under U. D. C.

I am now presenting as case studies the details of two documentation lists to give a clear idea of the method followed in compilation, work study, and the merit of the lists.

Case Study 1
Atomic Energy Establishment, Trombay

The Atomic Energy Establishment, Trombay (AEET) is the national center for research in and development of the peaceful use of atomic energy in India. The organization has planned to develop its Library Information Service as one of the leading libraries in the world in the field of nuclear science and technology.

The Library and Technical Information section has at present a collection of 127,280 research reports and other documents, mostly in the field of nuclear science and technology. The Library is the Depository Library in India for the USAEC research and technical reports. The Library also receives, through exchange, the research reports of various atomic energy organizations in the world, as well as those of international agencies such as CERN, EURATOM, IAEA, etc. Approximately 1,600 reports are added each month. To ensure fullest utilization of the scientific and technical reports received from the various atomic energy organizations, the Library issues a semi-monthly annotated documentation list Bibliography of Current Reports (BCR). The entries in the BCR are carefully selected from the point of view of the needs of researchers and they are indexed in two parts. Part 1 contains the conventional reports and Part 2 lists reports in microform. The entries are classified under broad subject headings as used by Nuclear Science Abstracts (NSA) and are provided with cumulated contents pages and report number.

A sample entry in the Bibliography of Current Reports is given below:

Health and safety including Dosimetry - General

7f: 1570 CONF - 650616. 28
   Evaluation of the Hazards from Radioactive Gas and Ozone at Linear Electron Accelerators
   George, Andreas C; et al.
   Oct. 1965, 54 p
   (CONF - 651109-18)

The citations are arranged in the following sequence

(1) Serial number, (the prefix attached to the serial number indicates the form in which the report is available); (2) Report number; (3) Title; (4) Author; (5) Issuance date, number of pages, language; (6) Cross reference number; (7) Annotations or Notes. The entries are arranged under the subject headings, and the class number is not given.

Titles of the majority of scientific and technical reports are explicit and so it was felt unnecessary to give abstracts. When the titles are not self-explanatory, annotations are provided.

Bibliographical Services in India   41

The basic purposes of this documentation list are to provide current awareness and to supplement the services, already available at the international level, of Nuclear Science Abstracts (NSA). The list attempts to bridge the time gap between the date of the receipt of the original document and the date of receipt of the issue of Nuclear Science Abstracts in which that particular document is abstracted. In India where research activities depend mostly on Western countries, and where it takes ten to twelve weeks from the date of issuance to receive the materials, such local documentation lists are very effective as a tool for current awareness. Retrospective searches are usually made from Nuclear Science Abstracts together with other comprehensive indexing and abstracting periodicals.

The BCR, though a selective documentation list oriented to the research activities of the Atomic Energy Establishment, is distributed to a number of other scientific institutions.

Selective Dissemination of Information

The Library and Information Service also maintains a record of the subject field of interest of individual scientists and different scientific divisions for carrying out selective dissemination of information for immediate communication of the literature of interest.

M. K. Raghavendra and V. A. Kamath made a study of work flow and staff time involved in the compilation of 500 entries in each issue of the BCR list. A team of eight, one professional, one semi-professional, five clerical and one tradesman, are engaged in the compilation and issuance of this documentation list. The time spent by each category of workers is as follows:

1. Classification officer (professional   38 hrs 18 min
2. Scientific Assistant (semi-professional)   11 hrs 35 min
3. Clerical   123 hrs 21 min
4. Tradesman   32 hrs --

The flow of work showing types of operations is presented in a chart on the following page.

Case Study 2
Indian Statistical Institute Library, Calcutta

The Indian Statistical Institute is an institution of national importance and higher learning in the country. The Library of the Insti-

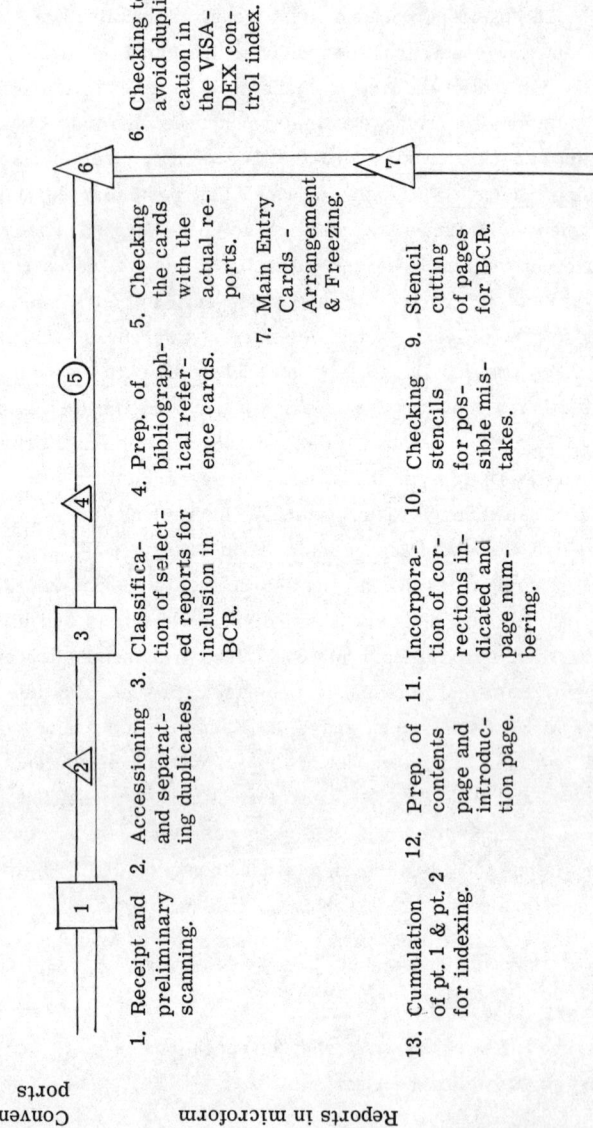

Work-Flow Chart Showing Types of Operations for the Compilation of BCR

Pt. 1. Conventional reports

Pt. 2. Reports in microform

1. Receipt and preliminary scanning.
2. Accessioning and separating duplicates.
3. Classification of selected reports for inclusion in BCR.
4. Prep. of bibliographical reference cards.
5. Checking the cards with the actual reports.
6. Checking to avoid duplication in the VISA-DEX control index.
7. Main Entry Cards - Arrangement & Freezing.
9. Stencil cutting of pages for BCR.
10. Checking stencils for possible mistakes.
11. Incorporation of corrections indicated and page numbering.
12. Prep. of contents page and introduction page.
13. Cumulation of pt. 1 & pt. 2 for indexing.

Bibliographical Services in India

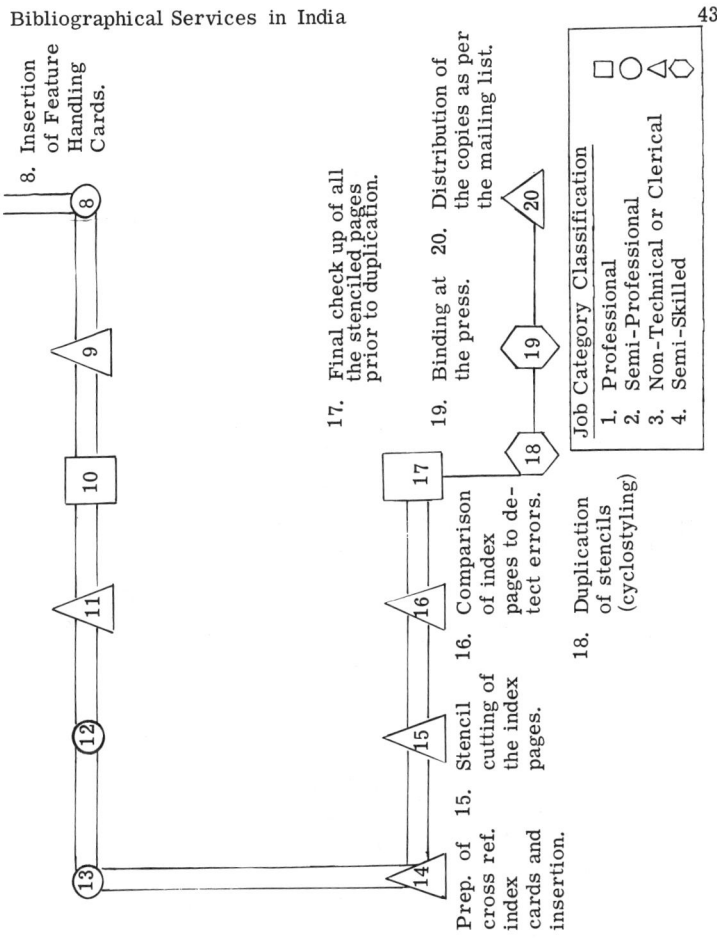

tute has a rich collection of 115,000 volumes and receives about 2,300 current periodicals in statistics and its allied subjects. The Library's bibliographical and documentation services include regular issuance of the Monthly Bulletin of Acquisitions and Library News and a documentation list, The Index to Statistical Literature.

The scope and coverage of this local documentation list are examined here. Each issue of this statistical index includes the articles on methodology in theoretical and applied statistics that appear in current scientific and technical periodicals received by the Library during the preceding fortnight. The index can claim to be very comprehensive as the Library receives all the important statistical and mathematical periodicals of the world as well as a large number of others in which statistical articles appear. About 650 periodicals of the 2,300 periodicals received in the Library are regularly scanned. Immediately on receipt of the periodicals the issues are carefully reviewed and the entries are typed, giving the necessary bibliographical details. In classifying the selected items on theoretical statistics the special classification scheme designed by the International Statistical Institute is followed. The articles on applied statistics are classified by a faceted classification scheme designed by the Indian Statistical Institute Library. The classified entries are then indexed under subject headings. Mimeographed copies are issued for internal circulation as well as to outsiders interested in receiving the index. The layout in double column permits use of entries on 3" x 5" cards, which are used also for maintaining the index on cards. Master cards are filed in the institute Library, one in author sequence and another in classified sequence, for retrospective searches and bibliographical service. A sample entry is given below:

    S1   Probability

        .1 calculus of probabilities

    CUPPENS, R.: Decomposition des fonctions
    caracteristiques indefiniment divisibles.
    Comptes Rendus des Seances de L'Academie
    des Sciences, Series A & B - v. 263, no. 18,
    November 2, 1966. p. 616.   (17751)

        .5 limit theorems

    CSISZAR, I.: On infinite products of random

elements and infinite convolutions of probability distributions on locally compact groups. Zeitschrift fur Wahrscheinlichkeitstheorie und Verwandte Gebiete - v. 5, no. 4, 1966. p. 279. (17767)

S 2 Frequency Distributions

.1 descriptive properties

*HUZURBAZAR, V. S.: Some invariants of some discrete distributions admitting sufficient statistics for parameters. Iowa State University of Science and Technology, Statistical Laboratory, Reprint Series; no. 175, 1963. p. 1. (17786)

* Indicates separate document.

The process of indexing and issuance of the list is designed so that there is rarely a time lag beyond four weeks from the date of receipt of the periodical in the Library. It must not, however, be forgotten that in India we depend mostly on foreign periodicals for advanced studies and research and it takes 6 to 8 weeks or more for periodicals to arrive by sea mail.

The number of articles indexed in the documentation list over a five year period is given in the table below. The number of articles on statistics reported in the INSDOC List during the same reference period is also given for comparison and to get an idea of its comprehensiveness.

Articles on Statistics reported in the Index to Statistical Literature and in the Insdoc List

Reference period	Insdoc List	ISI Index to Statistical Literature			Percentage	
		theoretical	applied	total	2/3x100	2/5x100
(1)	(2)	(3)	(4)	(5)	(6)	(7)
April 1960/March 1961	160	917	1458	2375	17.5	6.7
April 1961/March 1962	166	1274	1957	3231	13.0	5.1
April 1962/March 1963	187	1343	1263	2611	13.9	7.2
April 1963/March 1964	169	1306	1255	2561	12.9	6.6
April 1964/March 1965	189	1560	992	2552	12.1	7.4
Total 5 years	871	6400	6930	13330	13.6	6.5

The number of entries in the INSDOC List comprises only 6.5

percent of the number of entries in the Index to Statistical Literature, or 13.6 percent of the entries on theoretical statistics.

The Indian Council of Agricultural Research publishes the quarterly Statistical Newsletter and Abstracts for the research workers in agriculture and animal husbandry. 313 abstracts on statistics were published in the Newsletter from April, 1963 to April, 1965. The primary date of publication of 83 entries could not be ascertained either for non-occurrence of the month of issue in the publication or because the periodical was not in the ISI Library. The distribution of 230 entries by time lag is given in the table below:

Statistical Newsletter and Abstract, Distribution of entries by time lag in months

	0	1	2	3	4	5	6	7	8	9	10	11	12	total no. of entries	percentage
1-12 months								2	1					3	1.3
12 months+		2			6	9	3	29	13	4	24	13	5	108	47.0
24 months+	32	11	5	29	12	4	15	3	1	6				118	51.3
36 months+	1													1	0.4

Only 1.3 percent of entries are within the time lag of one year, 47.0 percent are beyond one year but within two years, 51.3 percent go back as far as three years and 0.4 percent go back as far as four years.

The coverage and the time lag between the date of publication of the article in the primary journal and the date of appearance in the Newsletter raises the vital question of current usefulness of the abstracting service at the local level.

The coverage and promptness of two abstracting periodicals on theoretical and applied statistics issued under the aegis of the International Statistical Institute are examined below.

In 1962 the International Journal of Abstracts; Statistical Theory and Method published 673 abstracts and the International Journal of Abstracts on Statistical Methods in Industry had 309 abstracts. Of 673 entries in the former, the date of publication of 451 articles could not be ascertained as the primary publications did not indicate the month of issuance. The time lag study of 222 entries (30.0 percent of the total) is presented in the table below:

International Journal of Abstracts; Statistical Theory and Method
Distribution of entries by time lag in months

	0	1	2	3	4	5	6	7	8	9	10	11	12	total no. of entries	per-centage
1-12 months					24			9	2	1	28	17	2	83	37.4
12 months +	20	7	4	23	3	3	15	6			10	4	2	97	43.7
24 months +	3	2		9	5		6	1			5	5		36	16.2
36 months +	3	1			2									6	2.7

37.4 percent of the entries are covered within one year. The time lag of 43.7 percent is more than one year but within two years; 16.2 percent are up to three years old and 2.7 percent are up to four years old.

Of 309 entries in the International Journal of Abstracts on Statistical Methods in Industry, dates of primary publication of only 90 entries (28.0 percent of the total) could be ascertained. The distribution of time lag is given below:

International Journal of Abstracts on Statistical Methods in Industry
Distribution of entries by time lag in months

	0	1	2	3	4	5	6	7	8	9	10	11	12	total no. of entries	per-centage
1-12 months	1		2	7		17	1	2	2	1			3	36	40.0
12 months +	1		4	2	2			2	5	3	10	2	2	33	36.6
24 months +	3	2	7		3		2							17	19.0
36 months +	2										1		1	4	4.4

40.0 percent of the entries are covered within one year. The time lag of 36.6 percent is more than one year but within two years; 19.0 percent are up to three years old and 4.4 percent are up to four years old

Quality Control and Applied Statistics is another abstracting periodical on statistics. It records about 450 abstracts in each volume. Of the 434 entries recorded in the 1964 volume, dates of primary publications of 393 entries (90 percent of the total) could be ascertained. The distribution of time lag is given in the next table:

Quality Control and Applied Statistics.
Distribution of entries by time lag in months

	months													total no. of entries	percentage
	0	1	2	3	4	5	6	7	8	9	10	11	12		
1-12 months	26	34	58	75	63	52	32	27	9	4	8	5		393	99.7

Based on the small sample for which publication dates were found, this abstracting service appears efficient and quite effective; all but one of the abstracts was published within eleven months from the date of appearance of the original article in the primary journal.

The Insdoc List indexes a very small percentage of the statistical literature generated in a year and the entries are indexed under broad subject headings. The specific indexing needs of any special group apparently cannot be met by any form of all embracing centralized index.

The Statistical Newsletter and Abstracts publishes an average of 160 abstracts each year. This is almost the same number of articles indexed in the Insdoc List. 98 percent of the abstracted articles are two to three years old; so this list too is not helpful for keeping up to date.

Of the three international abstracting periodicals on statistics, two are restricted to the application of statistical methods and one deals with statistical theory and methods. In the abstracting periodical Quality Control and Applied Statistics almost all the articles are reported within one year but in the other two periodicals about 38 to 40 percent are within one year and the rest carried over to two to three years. These abstracting periodicals are helpful for specific searches and for comprehensive survey of the literature on statistics but not for current awareness.

This comparative time lag study reveals that though abstracting services are perhaps more effective for searching, their time lag makes them virtually useless for current awareness service. On the other hand, the indexing services or local documentation lists issued by the special libraries, despite their limited scope, are quite effective in reducing the time lag and are significantly useful for current awareness service to scientists in their respective fields.

Bibliographical References

Bhatia, Mohan "Indexing and Abstracting Serices in India." Indian Association of Special Libraries and Information Centres. Special Publication No. 8, Sixth IASLIC Conference, 1965, p. 85-104.

Kamath, V. A. and Raghavendra, M. K. "Effective Documentation Services in Nuclear Science and Technology." Documentation Research and Training Centre Annual Seminar (1964), p. 364-378.

Raghavendra, M. K. and Kamath, V. A. "Dissemination of Current Scientific and Technical Information in the AEET." Annals of Library Science and Documentation, 13(3):119-124.

Rajagopalan, T. S. "Indian Scientific Documents and Their Bibliographical Organization." Annals of Library Science 9(2):68-83.

Saha, J. "Problems and Prospects of Bibliographical Organization and Scientific Information in India." Annals of Library Science 9(1):39-50.

4. Indian National Scientific Documentation Centre

After independence in 1947, the Council of Scientific and Industrial Research, established in 1942, gave high priority to developing a network of scientific laboratories in India. This accelerated scientific research activities in India and, as a corollary, demand for increased scientific information and active documentation service began to be felt. In this situation it was felt necessary to establish a national documentation center to supplement the limited library facilities available in various research institutions.

At the recommendation of the Advisory Committee appointed by the Government of India in 1951, the Council of Scientific and Industrial Research established the Indian National Scientific Documentation Centre (INSDOC) in 1952. INSDOC was placed under the administrative control of the Director of the National Physical Laboratory, and was assigned the following objectives:

1. To receive and retain all scientific periodicals which may be of use to the country;
2. To inform scientists and engineers of articles which may be of value to them by issuing a monthly bulletin of abstracts;
3. To answer specific inquiries from the information available in the centre;
4. To supply photocopies or translations of articles required by individual workers;
5. To be a national depository for reports of the scientific work of the nation, both published and unpublished; and
6. To be a channel through which the scientific work of the nation is made known and available to the rest of the world.

In order to fulfill the functions mentioned above Insdoc attempted, from the very beginning, to build up a rich collection of scientific periodicals and other research communications. To avoid duplication of research materials available in several older research libraries in the neighborhood, and to use its limited book budget judiciously, INSDOC assessed the resources available at the Indian Council of Agricultural Research, the Indian Agricultural Research Institute (both having good collections in agriculture and biological sciences) and the Library of the Director General of Health Services (for literature on medical sciences).

In view of the availability of scientific literature on these subjects INSDOC built up its collection on other subjects, especially mathematics, the physical sciences and their applications. Considering the limited financial resources in India, the policy of acquisition which INSDOC adopted is a very good example of cooperative acquisition.

INSDOC List of Current Scientific Literature

As most of the Indian libraries had no facilities to provide bibliographical service for current awareness, INSDOC assumed responsibility for informing scientists and technologists of current research results published in periodical literature, and initiated publication of a semi-monthly bibliographical bulletin under the title INSDOC List of Current Scientific Literature. The primary objective in bringing out the INSDOC List was to bridge the time lag between the publication of scientific periodicals in foreign countries and their receipt in Indian libraries.

To reduce this time lag to some extent the contents pages of selected foreign scientific periodicals were obtained by air mail for indexing in the INSDOC List. About 950 periodicals widely used by scientists and technologists were selected in consultation with specialists and also from a study of the frequency of citation of titles of periodicals.

INSDOC arranged to receive advance information of the contents of foreign periodicals either in microform or in printed form through the John Crerar Library (Chicago), the Centre de Documentation of the CNRS (Paris, the Department of Information of the Academy of Sciences (Moscow), the CSIRO (Melbourne), the Information Bureau of the DSIR (Wellington) and the National Diet Library (Tokyo). Contents of Indian scientific periodicals were secured immediately on publication of the periodicals. Only the articles and communications of fundamental and substantive research value were selected for inclusion in the index.

The entries were classified according to the Colon Classification, indexed under a subject heading, and then, usually, arranged under the name of the author. Each subject heading consisted of three parts--the colon class number, its equivalent UDC number, and the name of the subject in natural language. Each issue indexed about

2,000 articles, arranged in classified sequence under 250 subject headings.

The INSDOC List was well received by scientists and librarians as a current awareness tool. The INSDOC List also demonstrated the value of documentation activities and encouraged several special libraries to start abstracting and indexing services that were specially designed and adapted for the researchers attached to their particular institutions.

Later the local documentation services provided by different subject libraries became more forceful media for current awareness on specific subjects. Several local lists compared favorably in coverage and design and several analytical articles appeared in Indian library journals evaluating the INSDOC List with those subject lists.

In February, 1964 Dr. Harold Wooster, Director, Information Sciences Directorate, U.S. Air Force Office, Washington made a short trip to India to study the functioning of documentation centers and special libraries in the country. Dr. Wooster reviewed the INSDOC services, and particularly the INSDOC List. His analysis was published in the IASLIC Bulletin. He concluded that "the INSDOC List is bringing Indian scientists a sample (and I suspect a random sample) of the world's scientific literature, but that it cannot be relied upon to replace any conventional indexes now in existence.... It should either be expanded to cover a significant fraction of the world's scientific literature, or abolished, at least in its present format." In 1964, INSDOC decided to discontinue the INSDOC List.

Bibliography of Scientific Publications of South and Southeast Asia

The UNESCO South Asia Science Co-operation Office (SASCO) in New Delhi brought out the Bibliography of Scientific Publications of South and South-East Asia during the years 1949 to 1954. The purpose of this bibliography was to provide systematic control and to disseminate the scientific papers and documents published in India, Burma, Ceylon, Malaya, Indonesia, and Thailand. It was issued half-yearly and twelve issues had been published before INSDOC took over responsibility of this bibliography in 1955, changing it to a monthly publication. However, the scope of the bibliography, "a comprehensive record of the scientific literature" published in the periodicals literature of South and Southeast Asia, remained unchanged. From a selection of about 300 periodicals on science and technology published in this region, about 7,500 articles were indexed in the bibliography per year. In the absence of any other bibliography of national coverage, INSDOC made continued efforts to attain full coverage of Indian scientific periodicals. Evaluation of this bibliography found that 90 percent of the entries were of Indian origin. The entries were listed in classified sequence, using Colon Classification and making the classification co-extensive with the specific subject of the article, and 200 subject headings were added. Author and subject indexes were provided at the completion of each annual volume.

This bibliography remains the major source of information about research contributions published in Indian scientific periodicals. The increased number of entries each year reflects the growth of scientific literature in India from 1956 to 1964 (see the table at the end of this chapter). The list did not attempt to record articles by the Indian scientists published in foreign periodicals and it is estimated that about 20 percent of the total Indian research contributions are published abroad. When INSDOC decided, in 1964, to publish <u>Indian Science Abstracts</u> for dissemination of Indian scientific literature, the <u>Bibliography of Scientific Publications...</u> was discontinued.

INSDOC started publishing Indian Science Abstracts in January, 1965, because: (1) coverage of Indian scientific literature in the international abstracting services was inadequate and it was felt that a national abstracting service having comprehensive coverage of the output of the country's scientific literature, could serve as a feeder service to the international services; (2) there is a marked tendency among Indian scientists to publish their research results in foreign periodicals, and the total number of such articles in foreign periodicals is estimated at nearly 20 percent of the annual research contributions of the country. Scientists argued that articles published in Indian journals do not get due recognition internationally, because they either remain unrecorded in the international abstracting services or are listed very late. It was considered that the <u>Indian Sci-</u>

ence Abstracts, as a feeder service to the international abstracting periodicals, might solve this problem; and, (3) it was also felt that a comprehensive inventory of Indian works would help the policy advisers on science to locate the areas where more emphasis is necessary.

<u>Indian Science Abstracts</u> records all scientific communications published in India, as well as Indian research articles published in foreign periodicals. It is estimated that 450 periodicals, 2,000 patents, 300 standard specifications and 500 research reports and monographs in the field of pure and applied sciences are published in India every year. Original articles including short communications, review and informative articles published in scientific and technical periodicals or in the proceedings of conferences and symposia, monographs and other ad hoc publications, as well as patents and standards are recorded in <u>Indian Science Abstracts</u>. About 1,000 entries are recorded in each monthly issue of <u>Abstracts</u>. The entries are arranged in classified sequence using UDC and subject headings.

The abstracts are classified under 19 broad classes which are further subdivided under about 450 subclasses according to Universal Decimal Classification (UDC). The entries are then arranged alphabetically by author's name under subject headings and serially numbered. The title is given in English irrespective of the language of the original article. The language of the article, if other than English, is indicated after the title. The author index and Keyword index refer to the abstract by serial number. Since 1966 both these indexes have been computer-based. Annual author and subject indexes are also provided at the end of each year for easy reference.

A sample entry is given below.

        52 Astronomy . Surveying . Geodesy
523 Astrophysics. Cosmology. Universe. Space

    BANNERJEE A (Jadavpur Univ., Calcutta-32): Stationary spherically symmetric dust distribution in a steady state universe. Indian J Phys 1966, 40(5), 269-70 [sc]
    Some interesting features of the soln. given by Hoyle and Narlikar (Proc R Soc 1964, 278A, 465) regarding a stationary spherically symmetric distribution of dust in an outside space which approaches asymptotically the steady state conditions have been presented. It is shown that the conditions of fit at the boundary set a possible upper

limit to the dimension of the stationary, dust distribution. There is also a lower limit to the value of density of the matter distribution [DSRM]

Bibliography on Indian Education

Under contract with the U.S. National Science Foundation, INSDOC undertook compilation and publication of the annotated <u>Quarterly Bibliography on Indian Education</u> starting in 1967.

Bibliographic Service

One of the major services of INSDOC is compilation of bibliographies on specific subjects on demand. It does not attempt to compile a comprehensive or exhaustive bibliography on the subject sought but limits its work to providing a selected bibliography to meet the requirements of each inquiry. Normally, the search is limited to the last ten years.

The requests for bibliographical services come mostly from industries, research workers, professional practitioners, government departments, and foreign inquiries. The number of inquiries from small industries increased more than eight-fold in four years. This reflects the governmental drive to promote small industries and the measure of INSDOC services rendered during the industrialization of India.

INSDOC has a growing collection of periodicals but its own resources are too limited to fulfill the objectives of the center. However, there are several older scientific and technical libraries in India which have rich collections of retrospective files of important periodicals. The INSDOC is attempting to meet the major part of the demand for scientific literature from resources available in the country through effective interlibrary cooperation with other major libraries in the country. When the demand cannot be met from internal resources INSDOC attempts to get the material required from foreign documentation centers.

However, in the absence of an up-to-date union catalog of periodicals in the country the speedy location of the material is somehow hampered. The union catalogs that have been published in India are all out of date.

The first attempt to publish a union catalog of periodicals in

India was made by Stanley Kemp in 1918, and this was supplemented by the following union catalogs of periodicals

1. Asiatic Society of Bengal (Calcutta). Catalogue of Scientific Serial Publications in the Principal Libraries in Calcutta, compiled by Stanley Kemp, 1918.
2. Institute of Science (Bombay). List of Scientific Periodicals in the Bombay Presidency, 1931.
3. India, Ministry of Health. Union Catalogue of Medical Periodicals in the Libraries in Calcutta. 1933.
4. India, Meteorology Department. Catalogue of Periodicals in the Libraries of the Department, 1936.
5. The Union Catalogue of Learned Periodicals in South Asia vol. 1, Physical and Biological Sciences, compiled by Dr. Ranganathan, 1952. (This catalog still stands as the most comprehensive union catalog available in printed form.)
6. India, Council of Scientific and Industrial Research. Catalogue of Periodicals Available in CSIR Organizations, 1955.
7. India, Director General of Health Services. Union Catalogue of Medical Periodicals in Indian Libraries, by S. A. Chitale, 1956.
8. Indian Council for Library Development. Union List of Learned American Serials in Indian Libraries, 1966.

In 1959, INSDOC started a project for compiling a Union Catalogue of Periodicals. The response from contributing libraries in the country was very favorable. However, for some reason, the returns received from different libraries could not be consolidated promptly and issued in a printed form for use by other libraries. The entries have been transferred to cards and INSDOC is maintaining and updating the cards file of periodical holdings of the major libraries in the country for bibliographic control of periodical literature.

Bibliography of Indian Theses

The theses accepted by Indian universities for doctoral degrees are not usually published. Until recently, no systematic attempt was made to build up a national depository of doctoral dissertations or to compile a bibliographical record of them. There is no annual bibliography of the theses accepted by all universities.

INSDOC has, since 1955, included theses in both the INSDOC

List of Current Scientific Literature and Bibliography of Scientific Publications of South and South-East Asia. INSDOC is now attempting to build up a national depository of the doctoral theses accepted by Indian universities in the fields of science and technology and to publish an Annual Abstract of Science Theses. Besides bibliographical information The Centre plans to supply microfilm copies of theses to scientists and research workers on request.

Translation Service

There is a dearth of language specialists in the country and only a few libraries have facilities for providing translations from foreign languages. A number of competent linguists are attached to INSDOC, which also maintains a register or panel of foreign language translators who are willing to make translations in their spare time.

Requests for translations are registered in the Documentation Service Section and, when necessary, INSDOC procures the original document which is then passed on to the Translation Section for prompt translation service. When the translation is completed, the original and the translation are microfilmed and filed in the Centre for future use, and the full size copy is then sent to the Documentation Service Section for transmission to the scientist who requested the translation.

In the absence of translation facilities in most of the university and research libraries, the demand for translation service through INSDOC is increasing each year. INSDOC handles about 1,000 translations per year and, during the last 15 years, has built up a substantial collection of translated documents at the Centre.

Every month INSDOC sends a list of completed translations to the British Commonwealth Scientific Office (BCSO) for inclusion in the Commonwealth Index of Scientific Translations.

The Centre also maintains an alphabetical card index of BCSO translations and procures BCSO translations on demand.

Microfilming and Photoduplication Services

Only a few Indian libraries are equipped to provide copies of documents in microform or by other methods. INSDOC has microfilming facilities and other reprographic equipment and provides copies of scientific literature. It also procures microfilm or photocopies from abroad when the original is not available in the country.

In the course of its first ten years of operation (1952-1963), INSDOC demonstrated the importance of documentation services for increased research activities and industrial development in the country. The Director-General of the Council of Scientific & Industrial Research, based on this evidence of the value of documentation services, in 1963 raised the status of INSDOC from its subsidiary position in the National Physical Laboratory to that of an independent national center. In addition to its normal activities in providing bibliographic services, document procurement, and translations and document reproduction, the Centre is now charged with responsibility for developing the National Science Library, for establishing regional centers of INSDOC in four regions of the country, for compilation and maintenance of the union catalog of periodicals at regional and national levels, for technical assessment of CSIR Libraries, for promotion of Project Information Files in the CSIR Laboratories and for conducting training courses on documentation and scientific translation.

Because of distance, time lag, expenditure involved in borrowing books from other cities in India, and the unwillingness of some libraries to lend periodicals, it has not been possible to make full use of the large collections available in Calcutta, Bombay, Madras, Bangalore, Hyderabad and other cities. The Regional Centre of INSDOC at Bangalore, established with technical assistance from UNESCO, is part of a larger scheme to decentralize the documentation service in this sub-continent. This Centre, with a full complement of photocopying equipment, is located in the Indian Institute of Science which has a rich collection of scientific periodicals and research reports to serve as the base for bibliographical and document copying services. This Centre has also planned to utilize the scientific literature available in the region through interlibrary cooperation.

The Council of Scientific and Industrial Research decided that all the national laboratories should be project oriented and INSDOC has been made responsible for organizing their libraries to suit this trend. Senior teams from INSDOC visited the National Metallurgical

Laboratory, the Central Leather Research Institute, the Regional Research Laboratory in Jammu and Kashmir, and the National Aeronautical Laboratory at Bangalore. In each of these, the team worked out the pattern for the project information files and also drew up the work flow and the staffing pattern. The work of these teams is continuing at other laboratories.

National Science Library

The most important work INSDOC has undertaken is that of the organization and systematic development of the National Science Library. The National Science Library has been conceived as a network of science libraries in the country. The Library assumed responsibility for surveying present periodical holdings and monograph holdings in the complex of science libraries in the country, and for filling the lacunae by progressively subscribing for materials which, for one reason or another, are not being received in the country. The Library is also attempting to compile a union catalog of holdings in different science libraries for bibliographical purposes. It also seeks to make sure that there is, somewhere within the country, a copy of all significant scientific periodicals produced throughout the world, regardless of the language of publication. The Indian libraries are subscribing for not more than 10,000 titles. Of these about 3,000 titles, which are being received at INSDOC, form the nucleus of the National Science Library. It is hoped that in the course of the next five years the National Science Library will achieve the target of 15,000 titles. The National Science Library is also charged with collecting all the significant scientific literature published within India.

INSDOC has now undertaken a program to publish the serials catalogs of various important scientific libraries in the country. The Catalogue of Serials in the National Science Library lists 3,447 titles. The Catalogue of Serials in the Indian Agricultural Research Institute Library has 5,448 titles. The Catalogue of Serials in the Library of the Indian Institute of Science, Bangalore, the Catalogue of Serials in the Indian Statistical Institute Library, Calcutta, the Regional Union Catalogue of Scientific Serials: Medical Libraries in Delhi and the Regional Union Catalogue of Scientific Serials, Bangalore, each recording approximately 3,000 titles, have already been published. Other catalogs scheduled to be released soon are Union Catalogue of Scientific Serials of the Libraries of the Geological Survey of India Complex, and of the regions Delhi, Banaras, and Mysore. Work is also proceeding on a compilation of holdings in the Zoological Survey, the Botanical Survey, the Asiatic Society, the Jadavpur University, the Indian Association for the Cultivation of Science, the Bose Institute, and the Institute of Nuclear Physics, all in the Calcutta area. The Atomic Energy Establishment, the Tata Institute of Fundamental Research, the Textile Institute at Matunga, the University of Bombay, and other institutions with sizeable periodical and serial holdings will be included in a volume comprising the Maharashtra-Gujarat Region. The holdings of all the libraries of national laboratories within the CSIR complex will form a separate volume. The master plan includes a list of the holdings of libraries of industrial organizations in the private and public sectors in a separate volume, and consolidation of all the holdings in these various lists, using a computer, in the form of a union catalog of serials at the national level.

INSDOC is also attempting to maintain profiles of current research projects in universities and research institutions in India with a view to preparing annual reviews of work in progress in different subject fields.

The National Science Library also plans to have suitable reprographic facilities for dissemination of scientific materials.

Bibliographical References

Guha, Bimalendu "Preparation of an Indexing Periodical such as the INSDOC List." (Documentation Research and Training Centre Annual Seminar Volume, 1962, p. 229-234)

Indian National Scientific Documentation Centre. Annual Reports.

Kesavan, B. S. "Presidential Address." (Sixth Conference: Indian Association of Special Libraries and Information Centres, December, 1965.)

Ranganathan, S. R. (ed.) Documentation and Its Facets, 1963.

Wooster, Harold "Some Observations on INSDOC Services." (IASLIC Bulletin 10(1):6-15, 1965.)

Scientific Papers Published in Indian Periodicals from 1956 - 1964

year	A general science	B mathematics	C physics	D engineering	E chemistry	F technology	G biology	H geology	HX mining	I botany	J agriculture	JX forestry	K zoology	KX animal husbandry	L medicine	M useful arts	U28 meteorology	total
1956	17	148	292	602	529	364	94	151	18	310	681	73	254	233	1,730	179	55	5,730
1957	13	142	275	562	469	371	31	184	11	283	568	80	184	154	1,632	173	61	5,213
1958	17	172	197	556	538	587	78	114	26	367	631	64	236	222	1,775	118]	69	5,769
1959	11	235	202	507	542	697	78	133	29	314	733	58	370	255	1,891	98	70	6,366
1960	6	202	237	602	699	664	126	153	5	389	544	68	295	251	1,948	125	49	6,363
1961	5	301	199	596	692	622	163	168	44	376	609	189	334	254	1,909	29	56	6,645
1962	-	323	252	556	710	585	102	138	38	504	694	67	376	291	2,243	122	48	7,049
1963	5	321	347	628	890	660	125	152	40	477	967	93	539	344	2,317	138	100	8,143
1964	16	276	362	791	798	867	115	217	51	520	1,160	101	468	393	2,788	187	87	9,197

5. Defence Scientific Information Centre

The Scientific Information Bureau which has been in existence since 1958 as a Division of the Defence Science Laboratory was converted, in May, 1967, to the Defence Scientific Information and Documentation Centre (DESIDOC), under the Research and Development (R & D) Organization, Ministry of Defence. The mission of DESIDOC is to collect, collate, and disseminate scientific information to research scientists, armed forces, management people, and other users.

DESIDOC is organized into the following divisions or cells: Publications & Printing Division, Documentation Division, Translation Division, Information Surveys & Research Cell, and Special Cell.

Publication Division

R & D achievements, scientific information and new developments, in the country and abroad, are disseminated through the following publications.

1. <u>Defence Science Journal</u>. A quarterly publication with two half-yearly supplements. The quarterly issues publish original research communications and the supplements provide review articles. All branches of science and technology related to defence problems are covered in this periodical.

2. <u>Abstracts of R & D Projects</u>. An annual publication giving the summary of progress on research and development projects undertaken by the various R & D establishments and laboratories. The publication is intended to serve the interest of all users in Defence Services/Establishments. A supplement to the <u>Abstracts</u> containing progress on selected projects is also issued in August of each year as a classified publication.

3. <u>R & D Bulletin</u>. A publication to disseminate achievements of R & D Establishments/Laboratories to the user services and to apprise them of the trend of research and development carried out on various important defence problems. This too is a classified publication.

Defence Scientific Information Centre

The Bulletin was issued annually up to 1966. From 1967 the publication has been split into four parts: electronics; engineering, aeronautics and vehicles; armaments; and general sciences, comprising materials research, environmental research, medical, food and naval research, and training.

4. R & D Digest. A bi-monthly pictorial publication mainly intended for the Defence Services to keep them abreast of the latest scientific and technological developments in India and abroad, as well as of activities of the R & D Organization. The articles are written in popular style.

Documentation Division

The library of DESIDOC has a well balanced collection of 80,000 volumes and receives about 700 periodicals covering all branches of science and technology.

The Documentation Division actively scans and processes the information appearing in the scientific and technical literature received in the Library, for dissemination to the scientists and technologists attached to several Defence R & D Establishments/Laboratories located in different parts of the country. This Division issues the following publications:

1. DESIDOC List of Current Scientific Literature. A semi-monthly publication started in July, 1964, the periodicity changing to monthly in July, 1967. Articles and communications on problems of defence research and development are given emphasis in this list.

The bibliographical details of the entry follow a standard cataloging code. When the language of the original article is other than English, the translated title in English is given and the language of the original article is indicated after the title. The entries are arranged in classified order by Universal Decimal Classification (UDC). The subject headings used are not always in hierarchical order of the main classes of the UDC but are selected from the point of view of the researchers engaged in defense research and development.

Each issue of the DESIDOC List is provided with an alphabetical subject index. Keyword entries used in the index are selected on the basis of the usage of scientists.

Though the DESIDOC List is primarily issued for reference in

Defence R & D Establishment/Laboratories the List is circulated to about 250 scientific institutions and universities for wider communication.

2. New Developments in Military Devices & Equipment. A quarterly bulletin intended for the dissemination of the latest scientific, technological and psychological developments which are likely to be of interest to the Services as well as to the scientists working in the R & D organisation.

3. Current Trends in Defence Research and Development. A bimonthly news bulletin, highlighting the latest trends in the field of defense oriented research and development. It presents information gathered from current scientific journals received in DESIDOC.

Translation Division

DESIDOC has facilities for the translation of scientific and technical documents from Russian, French, German, and Chinese. Language classes in Russian and German are also held for the scientific workers attached to the organization.

Information Surveys & Research Cell

The Information Surveys & Research Cell of DESIDOC carries out surveys, analysis, assessment and reporting of information needs, activities and progress both within the country and abroad. It has issued the following publications:

(1) Scientific Information Agencies: their functions and management.

(2) Role of Scientific Publications in Serving Research Workers, Industry, Armed Forces, and the Public.

(3) A Survey of Scientific Literature and Information Activities in India (R & D) and Abroad.

Bibliographical References

DESIDOC News, vol. 1, no. 1, June 1967.

Rangra, V. K. and others "DESIDOC List of Current Scientific Literature." (Paper presented at the IASLIC Conference, Delhi, 1967.)

6. Indian National Bibliography

The most noteworthy bibliographical activity of post-independence in India is the publication of the Indian National Bibliography.

The Indian National Bibliography, started in 1957, records books, pamphlets, and other documents published in the country in English and in fourteen Indian languages. It is based on materials received in the National Library under the Delivery of Books and Newspapers (Public Libraries) Act of 1954. The following types of publications are, however, excluded from the bibliography: (1) Musical scores, (2) Maps, (3) Guides to text books, (4) Ephemeral literature, and (5) Periodicals and newspapers, except the first issue of a new title.

The A. L. A. rules for author and title, 1949, and the rules for descriptive cataloging in the Library of Congress are followed. The entries are printed in Roman script and in English so that they may be used outside India.

The National Bibliography is a classified bibliography, arranged according to subject. It is divided into two sections: general publications and government publications, including those of quasi-government bodies. Each section is divided into two parts: classified and alphabetical. In the classified sequence the full descriptive entries are arranged according to Decimal Classification. The colon number is also assigned to each entry. Under each specific subject the entries are arranged alphabetically by the names of authors. A shorter entry is given in the alphabetical part under the name of the author, short title, imprint, and class number. The entries in the classified section are arranged according to the Dewey Decimal Classification. The subject index follows the chain procedure developed in India by Dr. Ranganathan.

The Bibliography is provided with an exhaustive index of author, title, subject, series, etc. The Bibliography was originally a quarterly but it has been issued monthly since 1965. A cumulated annual volume is issued for the convenience of users.

The Indian National Bibliography included 30,283 publications during the first three years, i.e., 1958, 1959, and 1960, of which 9,801, i.e., 31 percent, were in English. The language distribution of the publications recorded in the National Bibliography during three recent years is presented in the table below to give a clearer picture of the output of Indian literature.

Indian literature recorded in the Indian National Bibliography during 1961-62 to 1963-64

	language	1961-62	1962-63	1963-64
1	Assamese	173	440	144
2	Bengali	2,043	1,574	1,666
3	Gujarati	966	891	1,037
4	Gurumukhi	764	276	309
5	Hindi	2,805	2,730	3,500
6	Kannada	411	619	784
7	Malayalam	696	599	613
8	Marathi	1,038	1,558	1,793
9	Oriya	189	188	691
10	Sanskrit	168	250	281
11	Tamil	886	862	1,143
12	Telegu	924	892	789
13	Urdu	432	281	336
14	English	9,361	9,202	11,256
15	Other languages	220	154	218
16	Total	21,076	20,516	24,569

It was natural that in the initial years publishers either did not know about their obligation under the provisions of the Act or failed to realize the value of getting their publications recorded in the National Bibliography. Though the figures given in the above table cannot be taken as the exact number of books published during the year, it appears clear that the proportion of English language publications has increased during the last three years.

Retrospective Bibliographies

Along with the compilation of the current Indian National Bibliography, the National Library has undertaken to compile fifty-six retrospective bibliographies on Indology. These bibliographies will cover significant publications published from 1900 to 1953. The fourteen language bibliographies are to be compiled by the Sahitya Akademi, while the others, the subject bibliographies, are to be compiled by the National Library. Bibliographies on Indian Botany, Indian Anthropology and Bengali Language and Literature have been published.

Bibliographical References

Anada, Ram H. N. and Venkatachari, P. N. "The Indian National Bibliography." (Indian Library Association, Journal 2(4):13-20, 1960.)

Ketkar, N. M. "Romanization in National Bibliographies: A case study of INB." (Library Herald 7(4):223-234, 1965.)

7. Documentation on Social Sciences

Social Science Research Centers

Despite the fact that the social sciences have developed greatly during the last two decades there has been no general survey of achievements and trends in the social sciences in India.

However, increased attention to teaching and research in several disciplines of the social sciences is evidenced by the fact that all 62 Indian universities have departments providing facilities for teaching and research in some fields of the social sciences. The central and state governments and the Research Programmes Committee of the Planning Commission are providing funds to the universities for social studies and for acceleration of social science research in general.

The government itself, through its own specialized agencies and institutions, is giving increased attention to research which is mostly applied in nature and has been designed to provide adequate data for the measurement of economic and social development in the country.

No attempt has been made by the social scientists to write trend reports and to record the history and progress of research in different disciplines of the social sciences such as sociology, social psychology; criminology; cultural and social anthropology; demography; economics, statistics; public administration; political science; international relations; international and constitutional law; economic and social history; human, economic and political geography. Nor has any attempt been made by the social scientists and documentalists to record systematically the social data made available in the process of numerous surveys and experiments.

The data on growth of the social science research centers in India have been quoted from Social Science Research Centres in South Asia: A Directory of Institutions, compiled by the UNESCO Research Centre on Social and Economic Development in Southern Asia in 1965, and from annual reports of several institutions. The major areas of social sciences covered by these centers and the year of establishment are given in the table below:

Growth of Social Science Research Centers in India

period	general (1)	social anthropology (2)	social psychology (3)	political science (4)	economics & statistics (5)	public administration (6)	education & social work (7)	total (8)	cumulative total (9)
Before 1900	1				1			2	2
1901 - 1910					1			1	3
1911 - 1920	1	1	1		2			5	8
1921 - 1930	2		1	3	4			10	18
1931 - 1940	2	1			3		3	9	27
1941 - 1946	1	2	3	1	5		1	13	40
1947 - 1950	3	2	1	2	9		3	20	60
1951 - 1960	12	12	2	3	32	2	2	65	125
1961 -	1			1	11	1	2	16	141
Total	23	18	8	10	68	3	11	141	

It may be seen that out of 141 recorded centers 28.4 percent originated before Independence and 71.6 percent after that. This clearly shows increased awareness of research activities in the social sciences in the last two decades.

Special Libraries on Social Sciences

Though increased attention has been given to research on certain disciplines of the social sciences, the centers are very small. 85.0 percent of the centers have fewer than 100 staff members, of whom an average of 41.0 percent are research personnel.

The libraries attached to the centers are very small and are inadequate to meet research needs. The next two tables give the size of these collections and the number of current periodicals received. It may be seen that 90 of these libraries, or about 64 percent, have a collection of less than 15,000 volumes and receive less than 300 current periodicals.

Though the average size, scope, and facilities of the research centers is not very exciting, there are a few institutions which are fairly large and have earned international reputations as centers for higher learning and pioneering research in the social sciences. Spe-

Size of the Library Collection in Social Science Research Centers in India

numbers	general	social anthropology	social psychology	political science	economics & statistics	public administration	education & social work	total
(1)	(2)	(3)	(4)	(5)	(6)	(7)	(8)	(9)
Less than 5,000	7	6	4	3	27	2	4	53
5,000 - 10,000	3	6	2		12	1	3	27
10,001 - 15,000	2			1	6		1	10
15,001 - 20,000	2	1			6		1	10
20,001 - 25,000					4			4
25,001 - 30,000	2							2
30,001 - 40,000					1		1	2
40,001 - 50,000	1				1		1	3
50,001 - 60,000								
60,001 - 70,000	1							1
70,001 - 80,000		1		1				2
80,001 - 90,000				1				1
90,001 -100,000	2				1			3
above 100,000					1			1
Depending on Univ. Lib. facilities		2		2	6			10
Data not available		2	2	2	3			12
Total	23	18	8	10	68	3	11	141

Number of Current Periodicals Received in Social Science Research Centers in India

numbers	general	social anthropology	social psychology	political science	economics & statistics	public administration	education & social work	total
(1)	(2)	(3)	(4)	(5)	(6)	(7)	(8)	(9)
Less than 50	6	9	4	3	16	1	4	43
50- 100	6	1	2		14	1	2	26
101- 200	2				13	1	2	18
201- 300	1	1			1		1	4
301- 400	2				2			4
401- 500	1	1			4		1	7
501- 600								
601- 700					3			3
701- 800	1				2			3
801- 900								
901-1000								

(1)	(2)	(3)	(4)	(5)	(6)	(7)	(8)	(9)
1001-1500				2				2
1501-2000	1							1
Above 2000					1			1
Depending on Univ. Lib. facilities		2		3	6			11
Data not available	3	4	2	2	6		1	18
Total	23	18	8	10	68	3	11	141

cial mention may be made of the Gokhale Institute of Politics and Economics (1905), the Indian Statistical Institute (1932), the Tata Institute of Social Sciences (1936). the Deccan College Post-Graduate and Research Institute (1939), the Indian Council of World Affairs (1943), the Indian Institute of Public Administration (1954), the Indian School of International Studies (1955), the National Council of Applied Economic Research (1956), the Institute of Economic Growth (1958) and the Delhi School of Economics (1959).

Abstracting and Indexing Services

Documentation service has been rendered in some of the research institutions and universities. The following is an account of some of the institutions where documentation exists in the form of compilation and restricted circulation of documentation lists which serve as a current awareness service to the parent institutions.

In 1952, UNESCO established the South Asia Science Co-operation Office in Delhi which subsequently changed its name to UNESCO Research Centre on the Social Implications of Industrialization in Southern Asia with headquarters in Calcutta. In 1961, the Centre again changed its name to the UNESCO Research Centre on Social and Economic Development in South Asia and moved to Delhi. One of its main objectives is to collect and disseminate information on social and economic researches undertaken in Southern Asia, and for this purpose the Centre has been publishing annually since 1952 the Social Science Bibliography. It includes research articles in English and French found in about 200 periodicals and books. The text part of the bibliography is arranged under subject headings taken from the classification system of the International Committee for Social Science Documentation, with some alterations. In addition to the usual bibliographic information, annotations and abstracts are provided where necessary. Author and subject indexes are also provided for easy reference.

The Centre also started issuing an abstracting periodical in 1952 under the title South Asia Social Science Abstracts which included abstracts of articles dealing with the social aspects of economic development. In 1958 this publication merged with the Southern Asia Social Science Bibliography.

Since 1956, the UNESCO Centre has been publishing another periodical, The Research Information Bulletin: Social Science Projects in Southern Asia, to record research completed and research in progress. This publication coordinates research activities in the country and stops wastage due to duplication of work. The Bulletin lists research projects undertaken by universities, independent research centers, government departments, and individuals. The list, giving names and addresses of researchers and research institutions, enables researchers to correspond with one another when necessary. The projects in the Bulletin are listed under 30 subject heads, and in some cases further sub-divisions have been made. The projects are arranged alphabetically by name of institution. In each entry a summary of the work, name of the researchers and research guides, date of commencement, probable date of completion, and funds made available are given. The Bulletin is provided with a subject index, a personnel index, and a geographical index.

Since 1963, the Delhi University Library has been issuing the mimeographed Documentation List: Social Sciences. This list is compiled from articles published in English in about 255 periodicals.

In the field of economics, the Delhi School of Economics, the Institute of Economic Growth, the Ministry of Finance, the Ministry of Industry and Supply, the Ministry of Labour, and the National Council of Applied Economic Research are engaged in documentation service. Except for the Institute of Economic Growth, these institutions issue documentation lists for the current awareness of their researchers. The documentation lists compiled by these institutions differ widely so far as compilation, presentation, and indexing techniques are concerned. The Institute of Economic Growth prepares cards of research articles for the use of the researchers attached to that institution. The National Council of Applied Economic Research has a data service on Indian industries.

In 1951, the Librarian of the Ministry of Labour and Employment began compiling a monthly documentation list covering articles on labor problems.

The Classified Catalogue Code, with additional rules for a Dictionary Catalogue Code, is followed for cataloging the entries; for classification purposes, the schedule of Labour Economics in Colon Classification has been redesigned. In subject headings, the chain procedure is followed from the first link to the last.

The entries in a monthly list were arranged in classified sequence; each number carried its own class number. In the alphabetical index, the class number was used as the index number until 1954. Later, it was decided to give a serial number to each entry and to use that number for reference in the alphabetical index.

The documentation list is issued in two parts; the alphabetical index in part 1 and the classified entries in part 2. In 1957, the lists of all the previous five years were cumulated and provided with an index. Since then, monthly issues have been cumulated at the end of each year and an annual volume is issued with a cumulated index.

There was a favorable response to the Bibliography of Labour Literature, 1951-1957, from social scientists, administrators, and librarians. This encouraged the Ministry of Labour and Employment to organize a systematic bibliographical service within the library, and bibliographies of several important topics have been completed for wider circulation, viz.,

1. Labour Literature: A bibliography, 1951-57. 1957.
2. Select Bibliography on Labour Problems. 1958.
3. Bibliography on Current Labour Problems. 1958.
4. Labour Literature: A bibliography. v. 2, 1958.
5. Labour Literature: A bibliography. v. 3, 1959.
6. Labour Literature: A bibliography. v. 4, 1960.
7. Bibliography on Wages, 1958.
8. Bibliography on Labour Relation. 1959.
9. Bibliography on Workers' Education. 1959.

10. Nanda and Abid Ali on Labour Problems. 1959.
11. Trade Unionism: A bibliography. 1959.

The entries in the bibliographies are classified according to the Colon Classification. The scehdules of the subjects covered in each bibliography were redesigned to meet the requirement.

The Indian Council of World Affairs, the Indian School of International Studies, and the Indian Institute of Public Administration have documentation services in the fields of political science and national and international affairs.

The Indian Council of World Affairs and the Indian School of International Studies bring out annually bibliographies such as Documents on India, and Documentation on Asia. The monthly card compilation for these services is a current awareness service.

The Library of the Indian Council of World Affairs has taken up the following documentation work.

1. Documents on Indian Affairs, 1960. An annual volume containing, in full text or in excerpts, speeches, statements, resolutions, white papers, and agreements from official and non-official sources indicating significant trends in the political, economic, and social affairs of India. It has been modeled on Documents on International Affairs (Royal Institute of International Affairs) and Documents on American Foreign Relations (Council on Foreign Relations).

2. Documentation on Asia, 1960. An annual classified bibliography of articles on Asia and documents concerning significant developments in political parties, public organizations, and governments in Asia. About 4,000 articles are listed in each volume.

3. Select Articles on Current Affairs, 1956. An annual subject bibliography of articles on international relations and regional studies appearing in about 200 English-language periodicals during the year of compilation.

4. Indian Books of the Quarter, 1954. This compact bibliography, which has been published in the India Quarterly since 1954, lists (with annotations) current Indian publications in the social sciences. About 504 publications are listed every year.

5. India and World Affairs: Select bibliography, 1958. This bib-

Documentation on Social Sciences 75

liography, published annually in International Studies, has two parts
The first part lists books, articles and documents on the foreign
relations of India; the second part lists works concerned with Indian
opinion on world affairs.

The Indian Institute of Public Administration issues a monthly
documentation list entitled Public Administration Abstracts and Index
of Articles. This publication covers all aspects of public administration and selects articles from about 450 periodicals.

The Delhi University Library, with the help of the Department
of African Studies, brings out a quarterly mimeographed documentation list entitled Documentation List: Africa for the use of scholars
researching on Africa. It selects articles in English and French from
about 300 periodicals received in the Library.

In the area of education, the National Council of Educational Research and the Ministry of Education bring out the mimeographed
Current Education Articles (1965-) and the printed Indian Educational
Abstracts (1955 -).

The Ministry of Law publishes a mimeographed monthly documentation list entitled Documentation of Law.

There is no comprehensive list of the local indexing and abstracting periodicals issued by the special libraries in the social sciences.

Seminars on Documentation in the Social Sciences

The subject of social science documentation has been dealt with
in some detail in professional circles during the last ten years. It
has formed the subject of several seminars and conferences and the
discussions have helped to clarify the issues and highlight the priorities in the tasks to be completed.

The Library Seminar on Research in the Social Sciences held
under the auspices of the Indian School of International Studies in cooperation with the Indian Council of World Affairs Library in 1959
considered the establishment of a social sciences documentation center at length and made the following resolution stating that:

4. It be a recommendation to the Sponsoring Authorities of the
seminar to promote the establishment of efficient documentation service in the Social Sciences, by various means including

41. the establishment of an Indian National Documentation Centre

for the Social Sciences;

42. the contribution, by the said centre, of information on current materials published in India to international abstracting periodicals in the Social Sciences;

43. the prompt publication of select national documentation lists in the Social Sciences, to get over the time lag inevitable in the appearance of exhaustive international abstracting periodicals;

44. the maintenance of efficient inter-library loan in Social Science materials;

45. the co-ordination and economic provision of translation of documents in the Social Sciences in foreign languages;

46. the supply of mechanically-reproduced copies of specific documents in the Social Sciences on demand to libraries and to individual research workers.

The follow-up of the seminar was rather disappointing because no institutional framework had been provided to implement the recommendations.

The Seminar on International Relations and Regional Studies held under the auspices of the Indian School of International Studies at Bangalore in 1962 recommended the establishment of a Central Library on International Relations, which was to be linked up with the work of the proposed Indian National Social Science Documentation Centre and operate along the lines indicated in the recommendations of the Library Seminar on Research in the Social Sciences in 1959. The Bangalore seminar, however, restricted its recommendations to bibliographical control for research in international relations only and suggested the preparation of the following:

1. Catalog of current publications published in India;
2. Catalog of doctoral dissertations in India;
3. Catalog of the National Library;
4. Catalog of official documents in India;
5. Index to periodical literature in international relations;
6. Index to the writings on history of modern India; and the
7. Index to the news in a major newspaper.

While the recommendations specifically related to international relations, the major projects for the proposed Social Sciences Documentation Centre included the compilation of a union catalog of periodical holdings in the field of the social sciences, publication of documentation lists, interlibrary loan service at the international level, translation of documents, and the provision for microfilming and other reproduction facilities.

The subject was pursued again at the Seminar on Bibliographical Organization and Control in India held under the auspices of the Indian Library Association in Calcutta in 1962. The seminar recommended "a decentralized system of coordinated services based on the principle of subject specialization in the field of social sciences" and for that purpose it listed thirteen agencies, which were to take up social sciences documentation for the whole of India. The seminar also recommended the setting up of a national body to coordinate and supplement the activities and programs of various special subject centers and a Policy Advisory Committee for methodological guidance.

The IASLIC Seminars

The seminar at Lucknow in 1964 and the conference at Trivandrum in 1965 held under the auspices of the Indian Association of Special Libraries and Information Centres (IASLIC) discussed in detail the state of social sciences documentation in India and set forth concrete proposals in the form of several resolutions.

The conference recommended that IASLIC should collect information regarding available resources on social science subjects and finished documentation and bibliographical work in universities, and in the government departments and institutions concerned.

Bibliographical References

Girja, Kumar "Library Development in India: Retrospect and prospect." (Paper presented to the Seminar on Social Science Research and Library Development in India - February 25-27, 1967, New Delhi, under the joint auspices of the Indian Council of World Affairs and the Indian School of International Studies.) 1967.

Indian School of International Studies, New Delhi Seminar on International Relations and Regional Studies. Proceedings. 1965.

Ranganathan, S. R. and Girja, Kumar (eds.) "Social Science Research and Libraries." Papers and proceedings of the Library Seminar on Research in the Social Sciences, New Delhi, January 2-4, 1959.

Saha, J. "Social Science Research Centres in India" (Paper presented to the International Conference on Comparative Research on Social Change and Regional Disparity Within and Between Nations with Special Reference to Southern Asia). 1967. 8 p. 3 tables.

UNESCO Research Centre on Social and Economic Development in Southern Asia, New Delhi Social Science Projects on Southern Asia.

UNESCO Research Centre on Social and Economic Development in Southern Asia, New Delhi Social Science Research Centres in South Asia: A directory of institutions, 1965.

8. Education in Library Science and Documentation

In 1910, the first center for training in librarianship in India was initiated by an American librarian, Mr. W. A. Borden, who was appointed by Maharaja Sayaji Rao Gaekwad of Baroda as the Director of the State Library Department in Baroda. This attempt, however, met with little success. In 1915, a second library school was organized at Punjab University, Lahore, by another American librarian, Mr. A. Dickinson. The school continued successfully till the partition of India.

Madras University, under the able leadership of Dr. Ranganathan, organized its first course leading to a Certificate in Librarianship in 1929, and it became a regular program in 1931. In 1937, the University converted the Certificate course into a one year post-graduate diploma course. Andhra University in Waltair started a diploma course in librarianship in 1935. In the same year, the Imperial Library (now the National Library), under the sponsorship of the government, organized a training course leading to a Diploma in Library Science. The course was discontinued in 1945 when Calcutta University decided to start a diploma course in library science.

In the 1940's, several Indian universities realized the need of starting formal education in library science. Banaras Hindu University in 1941, Bombay University in 1944, Calcutta University in 1946, and Delhi University in 1947 started post-graduate diploma courses in library science.

In later years, the demand for trained personnel increased with the growing number of libraries and several other universities decided to have faculties of library science. At present, twenty-six universities offer one-year courses in library science leading to a Bachelor's degree or a post-graduate diploma. Names of the university library schools and the dates of the beginning of the one-year courses (leading to a degree or a diploma) are as follows:

Aligarh (1958), Andhra (1935), Banaras (1942), Baroda (1956),

Bombay (1944), Burdwan (1964), Calcutta (1946), Delhi (1947), Gauhati (1966), Gujarat (1966), Jadvpur (1963), Jiwaji (1964), Karnatak (1963), Kerala (1961), Lucknow (1962), Madras (1937), Mysore (1965), Nagpur (1956), Osmania (1959), Poona (1956), Punjab (1960), Rajasthan (1961), Sagar (1962), Shivaji (1964), SNDT Women's University (1963) and Vikram (1957).

Of these twenty-six library schools, six universities began the course in the 1950's and fourteen started in the 1960's. During the last ten years, many universities have organized library science departments. Unfortunately, some of the new universities have started courses without adequate libraries and proper teaching facilities.

The University Librarian, in most cases, heads the Library Science Faculty of the university. The teachers are mostly drawn from the library staff for part-time teaching. Dr. Ranganathan was the first full-time Professor in Library Science appointed in Delhi University and taught from 1947 to 1955. Since then, several universities have appointed regular teachers in Library Science to do the major part of the teaching. However, some librarians still continue to teach on a part-time basis. There are, of course, a number of library schools continuing to be managed solely by part-time lecturers recruited from the working librarians.

P. N. Kaula in a recent paper, "An Evaluation of Education for Librarianship in India," has provided information on the size of library school teaching staffs.

School	Full-time	Part-time	Total	School	Full-time	Part-time	Total
Aligarh	2	2	4	Kerala	2	2	4
Andhra	1	4	5	Lucknow	1	2	3
Banaras	4	4	8	Madras	4	1	5
Baroda	-	4	4	Mysore	2	2	4
Bombay	-	4	4	Nagpur	2	3	5
Burdwan	-	3	3	Osmania	2	3	5
Calcutta	2	11	13	Poona	1	3	4
Delhi	5	3	8	Punjab	2	3	5
Gauhati	2	2	4	Saugar	2	1	3
Jadavpur	2	2	4	Shivaji	1	2	3
Jiwaji	2	-	2	SNDT	-	4	4
Karnatak	-	6	6	Vikram	3	-	3

As one can see from the above table, the larger percentage of library school teachers are working librarians teaching on a part-time basis.

Further, due to small teaching staffs, very few schools can afford tutorial services, group discussions, field observations, and experimental work. The students get little opportunity to use the library as a laboratory for experimental work; thus, there is very little integration of theory and practice.

Library education in India is still aimed at producing library workers capable of handling routine library jobs, i.e., library technicians and not scholar librarians. In these teaching oriented library schools practically no attention is given to raising the intellectual standards of the courses and encouraging research activities. None of the university library schools is provided with funds for long range research in library science.

The full-time teachers have heavy teaching loads and thus have little time for research. There is also very little coordination of research activities in Indian library schools.

Delhi University and Banaras University have initiated a two-year post-graduate course leading to a Master's degree in Library Science. The University of Madras laid down the necessary regulations and syllabus for this course in 1960, but it could not start the course earlier than the 1967-68 academic year. The M. Lib. Sc. course of the three universities conforms more or less to a single pattern formulated under the guidance of Dr. Ranganathan. This advanced course covers a few aspects and methods of documentation, but it is only one of many optional subjects. At the graduate level of training, there are, however, significant variations in the admission requirements, curriculum and syllabus, and in the teaching methods followed by different universities.

In the curriculum, the solid core consists of courses in theoretical and practical classification, theoretical and practical cataloging, library organization, and library administration; book selection, physical bibliography, document bibliography and reference service are offered in a variety of combinations.

In order to achieve uniformity in curriculum and to improve

the standard of education, librarians and teachers of library science have met in a number of seminars in the last ten years. In 1961, the University Grants Commission appointed a Review Committee to consider the question of improving the standards of teaching and research in the departments of library science of the universities. The Committee examined with great care the training courses offered by different universities and other associated problems and in the report Library Science in Indian Universities (University Grants Commission, New Delhi, 1965) recorded the following findings:

> There is no uniformity in regard to the pattern of papers, admission qualifications, scope of practical training, quality of teachings, etc. There is an urgent need for improving standards of teaching and research in the departments of library science in the universities. The pattern of library education which has evolved in the country is not quite suited to the requirements of the new environment that has developed. The problems which have now to be faced will have to be tackled boldly after a systematic investigation, if library education has to develop along right lines in the future.

The Committee then made certain recommendations which would bring about uniformity in curriculum, teaching methods, and admission requirements, thus raising the standard of education.

In view of the recommendations of the Review Committee of the University Grants Commission mentioned above, the Delhi University Department of Library Science organized in September, 1966 a seminar on the teaching of library science in India. The seminar discussions were aimed at a critical and comprehensive evaluation of teaching in library science with a view to exploring ways of correlating it with the increased demands of higher education and research in India. The major recommendations of the seminar are as follows:

1. The Seminar places on record its indebtedness to the excellent document on "Library Science in Indian Universities" drawn up by the UGC Review Committee and for making a number of valuable recommendations on which the present Seminar has drawn heavily and fruitfully during the course of its deliberations. The object of the present Seminar has been to make adequate provision for implementing some of the basic recommendations of the UGC Review Committee,

Education in Documentation

by putting them in a perspective and in the context of contemporary librarianship. The recommendations of the Seminar attempt to give a reorientation of the approach, without in any way reducing the intellectual content of the courses spelled out in the UGC Committee Report, by providing scope for broad-based and specialized training in various areas of professional work.

2. B. Lib. Sc. Programme

The courses at the B. Lib. Sc. level should provide a balanced and well-rounded training, integrating theory with practice, and covering with equal emphasis all aspects of professional work. The courses offered should reflect the present needs of libraries. The following steps are suggested for improving the existing training programmes:

1. Stiffening entrance requirements;
2. Attracting students with higher academic qualifications, by offering suitable incentives;
3. Limiting the number of students admitted and maintaining the student-teacher ratio as recommended by the U. G. C. Committee;
4. Enlarging the contents of the courses by the addition of two more papers on literature studies in the fields of Sciences, or Social Sciences, or Humanities, and combining some of the existing papers such as classification theory and practice, cataloguing theory and practice, organisation and administration, etc., without diluting their contents by increasing the work load of students accordingly, so that the additional courses could be covered within the academic year, or by extending the duration of the course from 9 months to 12 months;
5. Integrating theory with practice; providing experience in field conditions;
6. Reconsideration of the present methods of examination and assessment;
7. Insistence upon practical library experience for teachers of library science. It should be possible for teachers to participate in actual library work for specific periods;
8. Establishing a closer and integrated participation of University Library and Departments of Library Science;
9. Involving qualified practicing librarians also in the teaching of students whenever feasible;
10. Utilising the services of members of other faculties in the University for handling special subjects.

Starting of new schools for B. Lib. Sc. should be done only after a careful study of the actual demand in the field and the availability of adequate training facilities including competent teachers.

3. M. Lib. Sc. Programme

The M. Lib. Sc. Course should provide scope for specialisation in a wide range of subject fields. It can have a minimum number of "required" courses and offer a wide choice of optional papers from a variety of courses. It should be possible to fit the program to the needs of the individuals, by providing or by making provision for a custom-tailored approach. The optional papers could be in the fields of advanced classification, or advanced cataloguing, or documentation, or information retrieval theory, bibliography, business libraries, government libraries, public, academic, research and school librarianship, or in any area of the subjects of librarianship in a contemporary form. In addition, there should be a dissertation based on research or investigation. The M. Lib. Sc. Course could form an intermediary stage for pursuing research at an advanced level leading to a Ph. D. The other factors to be considered for maintaining a high standard of training are:

1. Extremely careful selection of students for admission to the course;
2. Limiting the number of students to be admitted, maintaining the student-teacher ratio as recommended by the U. G. C. Committee;
3. Provision of competent personnel with field experience for teaching M. Lib. Sc. Course;
4. Securing the services of members of other faculties in the University for the teaching of special subjects, whenever necessary;
5. Provision of adequate facilities and resources for maintaining the training programme at a high level.

The reorientation of the training programme suggested above should be experimented upon by the existing schools offering the M. Lib. Sc. Course at present.

Starting of new schools for M. Lib. Sc. should be broached with great caution and only after careful consideration of the actual demand in the field, and the availability of adequate training facilities including competent teachers.

Education in Documentation

4. Research Programme

The Seminar supports fully the areas for research spelled out in the U. G. C. Report. In addition, it recommends that library schools should actively take up research on library problems faced by libraries in their day to day operation. These problems could be tackled as assignments at B. Lib. Sc. level, or as projects at M. Lib. Sc. level, or research level, depending on the nature of the problems. Thus the library schools could actively involve themselves with the library problems. For some of the problems which require interdisciplinary competence, the assistance of specialists in the various fields should be sought for guiding the research work. The research programmes should embrace all aspects of library science. The problems can be broadly divided into (1) pure research; (2) practical or applied research; or (3) developmental work.

Research programmes have to be developed on the basis of availability of guides with adequate technical competence and maturity. Admission of a candidate for research work should also take into consideration the fields of specialisation as well as the competence of a candidate for that particular work. It is recommended that the universities should gradually build up the research competence of the teaching staff of their faculty members by providing them opportunities for advanced training in their fields of specialisation. The research programmes of a Department should necessarily be built around such competent persons. In all cases where guidance from other Departments of the universities is required, it should be made available for the conduct of research in the Department of Library Science. The Departments should provide fellowships for research workers.

Besides the instruction in Librarianship offered by the Universities at graduate level, several Universities and the State Library Associations conduct training courses of varying length and depth and award certificates on successful completion of the training. The subjects taught are the same as for the diploma or degree course, but at an elementary level.

Training in Special Library Methods and in Documentation

The need for expansion of scientific library and documentation services to integrate the scientific information and bibliographical work with different stages of activity in scientific research and experimental design has now been realized as essential to the developments in science, technology, and industry. The increased demand for deeper analysis in indexing and the capabilities of machines for quickly handling and processing a large volume of microliterature have actively engaged the minds of scientists as well as of librarians. Despite the fact that several active groups under the guidance of Dr. Ranganathan began to give systematic thought to this new discipline emphasizing the need of research on the design and capabilities of indexes, faceted classification, indexing by chain procedure, correlative indexes and experimentations on several aspects of alphabetical indexes, the entire field of this new subject (documentation) remained in a somewhat chaotic state due to the lack of systematic training facilities for this new professional--the documentalist. The failure to recognize the importance of formal training in documentation arises partly from the failure of the profession to define what documentation is and, therefore, what kind of training is necessary.

The personnel needed for documentation work continued to be recruited from the ranks of subject specialists or personnel trained in library science. But the dearth of trained personnel for documentation work and their lack of adequate training in documentation methods remained a great handicap in documentation work.

The Indian National Scientific Documentation Centre (INSDOC), recognizing the need for special training in documentation, organized several in-service trainings for the special librarians working in different libraries and information centers. Such practical training generally extended for a period of six to eight weeks.

The Indian Association of Special Libraries and Information Centres, (IASLIC) established in 1955 on the model of ASLIB in the United Kingdom, gave some thought to the training of the special librarians and documentalists. The Committee appointed in 1958 for organizing a training program submitted a scheme and also drafted the curriculum for the training course. In the absence of sufficient encouragement and financial support, the training course could not be started earlier than 1966. Details of the course now conducted by the IASLIC have been given separately.

In a paper published in the Annals of Library Science in 1959, Dr. Ranganathan outlined a syllabus and the course training for documentalists. In the detailed scheme, Dr. Ranganathan mentioned that it would be useful to form special groups at higher technical educational establishments to train documentalists. As the training would be at a sufficiently advanced level it has been laid down that a candidate for admission to the course should have an M. A. or M. Sc. or Honours degree preferably having familiarity with bibliographic work and service. The training would last for one year and the course of studies has been designed to provide training in the thematic working plan of the documentation service at scientific research institutes: search, selection and evaluation of printed works and other technical information material and systematization of this literature with the aid of depth classification and methods of literature search. This syllabus received wide attention and the appreciation of many, but unfortunately none of the universities could implement it and reorganize the existing training in library science to cover the training of subject bibliographers and documentalists for financial and other reasons.

While drafting the proposals for the Second Five-Year Plan (1956-1961) for India, Professor P. C. Mahalanobis, F. R. S., Director of the Indian Statistical Institute and a member of the Planning Commission, became aware of the growing importance of documentation service for pertinent data and information. In 1956, he invited Dr. Ranganathan, who was at that time in Zurich, to return to India and organize training in documentation under the sponsorship of the Indian Statistical Institute. Dr. Ranganathan contended that since the rate of growth of scientific research is slow and industrial output was small and also, since most of the researches depended on western literature and technical know-how, the country was not sufficiently mature to accept documentation as an independent technology. The situation, however, changed very much in the next five years' time and in 1961 the Indian Statistical Institute inaugurated the Documentation Research and Training Centre (DRTC) in Bangalore, headed by Dr. Ranganathan.

Documentation Research and Training Centre (DRTC)

The objectives of DRTC have been expressed in the following terms:

1. To train documentalists for service within India and also to extend these facilities to documentalists needed in other countries, particularly in the fast-developing Afro-Asian countries; and
2. To organize continuing research on documentation.

Training

DRTC offers comprehensive instruction in the theory and practice of documentation. For this purpose it emphasizes

1. Imparting theoretical knowledge of a high order;
2. Equipping students with the necessary professional competence based on practical experience; and
3. Developing in the students the power of systematic thinking and exposition.

DRTC has made provision for:

1. A well-balanced advanced course of studies;
2. Project work;
3. Apprenticeship;
4. Observational field study;
5. Colloquium; and
6. Annual seminar
7. It adopts the Discussion Method and individual instruction in imparting theorectical knowledge.
8. The course continues for fourteen months (340 working days) in DRTC with six months extra being scheduled after the formal course for the completion of a project in the survey of trends in current literature.

Course of Studies

The DRTC course of studies has been designed to provide training in the thematic working plan of the documentation service at scientific research institutes: search, selection, and evaluation of documents and systematization of those documents with the aid of depth classification, and methods of literature search. The subject of study includes the following:

1. Universe of subjects, its development and structure;
2. Depth classification (Theory);
3. Depth classification (Practice);
4. Library catalog;
5. Documentation;
6. Research and technical library system.

Education in Documentation   89

A study of the history of sciences, an acquaintance with scientific literature, and a knowledge of the bibliographical tools in selected subjects, form an integral part of the course.

Project Work

Two projects have to be completed by each student, one during the formal course and the other after the final examination.

Project 1 is the compilation of a documentation list. Each student is assigned a particular subject of interest. He selects the host documents of micro-documents on that subject and prepares a scheme for abbreviating the titles of the host documents. He collects micro-documents published within a definite period from host documents; designs the depth schedule following the methodology of designing an analytico-synthetic scheme of classification by blending an a priori and a pragmatic approach; applies his schedule for classifying his collected documents and finally prepares a properly indexed classified documentation list supplemented by an author index and an index of class index entries.

Project 2 is the preparation of a trend report based on the survey of current literature on an assigned subject. Steps to be followed for the preparation of this report are more or less the same as those for Project 1. But in this report the text portion consists of linked up abstracts of different micro-documents giving reference to the documents cited in the author index, and in classified sequence with necessary subject headings.

Apprenticeship

A student admitted to the course is required to work as an apprentice for the first two months as well as during the last two months. The first term is known as pre-course apprenticeship and the last one as post-course apprenticeship.

Pre-course Apprenticeship

The pre-course apprenticeship covers the following:
1. Fairly wide reading of literature in each major subject field so as to sense the landmarks in its evolution and corresponding classics;
2. General orientation in various aspects of library management and services;
3. Becoming familiar with:

1. Reference books;
2. Bibliographies, including documentation periodicals;
3. Periodical literature in general;
4. Trade catalogs, lists, etc.;
5. Work of procurement of documents in a library and in a documentation center; and
6. Make-up and use of library catalogs.

Post-course Apprenticeship

Each student is required to obtain a good working knowledge of the following during his post-course apprenticeship:

1. Procurement of documents for a bibliographical center;
2. Preparation of subject bibliographies;
3. Document reproduction methods;
4. Translation service;
5. Machine methods of information processing and retrieval, using punch, sorter, collator, reproducer, tabulator and computer;
6. Compilation of the union catalog and methods of keeping it up-to-date;
7. Steps connected with the production of a documentation periodical; and
8. Form, make-up, classification, indexing and servicing of patents, standards, and similar documents.

Field Study

In addition to the apprenticeship periods, the students are given an opportunity to visit and observe the working of special libraries. They are, then, to submit critical reports of their observations.

Colloquium

Colloquia are held each week under two series:

1. Lecture series; and
2. Discussion series.

Lecture Series

In the Lecture Series, some expert in a particular field of interest is invited to give a lecture on his subject. The lecturer aims at giving a general view of the subject. The participants are then allowed to ask questions in order to get a clear understanding of the points covered by the lecturer. Each student, by turn, has to work as a rapporteur to a colloquium and to submit a detailed report for the record and a summary report for the press. This series is held during the first few months of the course.

Discussion Series

The scope of this series is usually confined to the subjects of

Education in Documentation 91

study in DRTC. In this series a student has to take the lead. The leader selects his topic and circulates his propositions (along with a bibliography on the topic) among the other students at least one week before the date of the colloquium. The colloquium begins with a formal introduction of the topic by the chairman. The leader, then, presents his propositions. Each student has to participate in the discussion. Those in favor of a proposition answer "for;" those not in favor answer "against. " The chairman conducts the colloquium according to the Rules of Procedure for Colloquium. Finally, a proposition is adopted as-it-is or in an amended form, as the case may be. The rapporteur submits a detailed report for the record and a summary report for the press. This series follows the lecture series and continues up to the end of the course at DRTC.

Annual Seminar

An annual seminar on some specified area of documentation is normally held in December every year. The seminar is open to the documentatlists of India and other countries. Students of DRTC should attend the seminar and, if possible, contribute papers.

The following subjects were discussed at the last four annual seminars.

1. (1963) Documentation periodicals: coverage, arrangement, scatter, seepage, and compilation.
2. (1964) Classification in document retrieval; subject heading in document retrieval; presentation of information.
3. (1965) Design of depth classification; standard for subject heading.
4. (1966) A recommendation for the use of a documentation list at the local level; design of depth classification; universe of knowledge; its structure and development.
5. (1967) Classification, subject headings, and management of reprography service.

Discussion Method of Teaching

Normally, the teachers in DRTC use the discussion method in teaching. Unlike in the lecture method, in the discussion method, the student participates actively instead of just listening.

Special Course

DRTC may admit officers already working as documentalists either for a refresher course, an advanced course, or for research in special fields in documentation. Details of such special courses are determined from time to time by the teachers of DRTC.

Research

The members of DRTC are continuously engaged in research on various problems of documentation. Some of the problems on which considerable progress has been made are:
1. Methodology for designing an analytico-synthetic scheme of classification;
2. Designing of depth classification schedules for subjects going with various basic classes;
3. Designing of comprehensive schedules for common personality, matter, and energy isolates; and
4. Methodology for the construction of subject headings.

Training Course in Documentation and Reprography offered by INSDOC

The number of students that could be trained by DRTC remained very limited. Considering the need for a larger number of trained documentalists, INSDOC, in 1964, decided to start a twelve-month training course in documentation and reprography. The course emphasizes practice as well as theory. The training is given at the postgraduate level. Except in the case of deputed candidates from national laboratories and research institutions, the admission requirement is a Master's degree.

In the first term, the students are given a general orientation in library science with a slant on special libraries, covering all the disciplines of classification, cataloging, reference service, bibliography, organization, and administration.

In the second term, instructions are given on the development of the pattern of knowledge and advances, classification, and cataloging. In the third term, the students deal with the evolution of the concept of documentation and its development and organization. In this term, the students are also given instructions on techniques of documentation. In the fourth term, the students are given instructions on the modern methods of information storage and retrieval and the techniques of reprography. Each student is assigned a project at the beginning of the second term which runs through all the remaining terms.

In the curriculum for training, the following subjects are cov-

ered in eight papers:
1. Organization and administration of special libraries
2. Reference service and bibliography
3. Pattern of knowledge and classification
4. Cataloging
5. Documentation--organization
6. Documentation techniques
7. Modern methods of information storage and retrieval
8. Reprographic methods

INSDOC also runs a training course in scientific and technical translation. Considering the increased demand for scientific and technical translations, INSDOC felt the necessity of organizing this separate course. The course aims at training technical translators, who will be engaged in research institutions and laboratories as staff translators. The six-month course is divided into lectures and tutorial sessions.

IASLIC Course

A training course in Special Librarianship and Documentation is offered by the Indian Association of Special Libraries and Information Centres.

Since 1966, the Association has been running this training course in Special Librarianship and Documentation. Admission is restricted to graduates with a degree or diploma in library science and working in special, academic, and research libraries.

In the curriculum for training the following subjects are covered:
1. Research and Technical Library Services
2. Depth Classification (theory and practice)
3. Cataloging and Indexing (theory and practice)
4. Documentation and Bibliographical Services
5. Information Service
6. Reprography and Translation Services

Each trainee is also assigned a project in the subjects listed in Items 2, 3, and 4 above.

Bibliographical References

Delhi University, Department of Library Science. Seminar on the Teaching of Library Science, September 2-4, 1966.

Hintz, Carl Education for Librarianship in India. Urbana, University of Illinois, 1963.

Kaula, P. N. "An Evaluation of Education for Librarianship in India" (UNESCO Bulletin for Libraries 21(4):182-189, 1967).

Indian Association of Special Libraries and Information Centres. Training Course in Special Librarianship and Documentation, Prospectus and Syllabus, 1966-67.

Indian National Scientific Documentation Centre Training on Documentation and Reprography, Prospectus, 1966-67.

―――― Training Course in Scientific and Technical Translation, Prospectus and Syllabus, 1966.

Indian Statistical Institute Documentation Research and Training Centre--Training in Documentation, Prospectus and Syllabus, 1967-68.

Ranganathan, S. R. "Course of Training for Documentalists" (Annals of Library Science 6:92-97, 1959).

―――― "Education for Documentalists" (Library Science with slant to Documentation 3(1):42-51, 1966).

―――― "Vitalising the University Education of Libraries" (Library Science with a slant to Documentation 3(4):293-315, 1966).

University Grants Commission Library Science in Indian Universities (Report of the University Grants Commission Review Committee). New Delhi, 1965.

9. Research in Library Science

While library education in India was formalized at the university level in the late 1930's, the curriculum remained at the library technician level; it was designed to train for routine library jobs rather than producing scholarly librarians who would be able to contribute to the development of library science. There is little scope or encouragement for research activities. None of the library schools at the university level have funds for research projects or experimental work. This is due primarily to the educational system of the country, and is partly due to dependence on Western countries for technical know-how. Though the overall picture is not very encouraging, the research contributions of Dr. Ranganathan in library science in general, and in classification in particular, gained a very distinguished position for the Indian school of thought. Dr. Ranganathan worked single handed for many years, using the Madras University Library, where he was the Librarian, as his laboratory for experimentation and research. He developed new concepts and a methodology which gained him international recognition.

Dr. Ranganathan in 1963 wrote that the starting of research in classification in India may be said to have been the formulation, between 1928 and 1930, of the "Five Laws of Library Science." The Laws based the entire edifice of library practices on normative principles.

His <u>Colon Classification</u> (1933), which appeared about the same time, had roots running deeper than the schemes of classification themselves. The ideas developed in Dr. Ranganathan's <u>Prolegomena of Library Classification</u> (1937) gave a great stimulus to further investigation into the problems of classification. His concept of five fundamental categories (PMEST) Personality, Matter, Energy, Space, and Time in his <u>Library classification: Fundamentals and Procedure</u> (1944) furthered this development. Dr. Ranganathan himself said that these ideas favored classification research but were only the very beginnings of systematic research in this field.

In 1948, the provision of a postgraduate degree course in the Department of Library Science at Delhi University created an ambiance in which Dr. Ranganathan could program systematic research in classification. In 1951, he established the Library Research Circle in Delhi and gave a detailed exposition to his thoughts on classification research in two monographs--Philosophy of Library Classification and Classification and Communication. The Library Research Circle attracted several intelligent and scholarly young men who studied classification problems in a more systematic and continued way under the guidance of Dr. Ranganathan. The research results and experimental design derived from the PMEST concept appeared in Abgila (the Annals and Bulletin of the Indian Library Association) and in Annals of Library Science. They were later consolidated in the book, Depth Classification (1953).

Later in 1951 Dr. Ranganathan, when working with this research group, conceived the idea of dividing the work of design and development of schemes for classification into three planes: "the idea plane," the "verbal plane," and the "notational plane." According to this approach, classification, when guided by the postulates and principles for the three planes of work, involves the analysis of the subject into its facets in the idea plane, transformation into standardized terminology in focal terms, in the verbal plane, and then translation into focal numbers in the notational plane according to the scheme of classification, followed by synthesis of the focal numbers into the class number.

In the idea plane the work essentially consisted of the delineation of the structure of the universe of subjects, sensing the modes of its development, recognizing the kinds of relation among the constituents of the subjects, and postulating about the pattern of relation and helpful sequence among the constituents. Dr. Ranganathan's work in the idea plane concerns the intrinsic attributes of the universe of subjects. He evolved the concept of the spiral of scientific method for deeper analysis of the process of classification. The postulational method has helped colon classification to advance from being a rigidly faceted classification to a freely faceted one.

At the verbal plane a set of standard terms has been developed over the past 30 years--from the time of the first edition of Prolegomena in 1937--to permit proper understanding of the contributions made in the area of classification. The Documentation Sectional Committee of the Indian Standards Institution prepared a glossary of classification terms and a glossary of cataloging terms which are a very useful contribution for understanding the Indian school of thought in the field of classification and cataloging. Further revision of the terminology has been included in the third edition of Dr. Ranganathan's Prolegomena (1967).

At the notational level Dr. Ranganathan worked to formulate the normative principles so as to create a "Grammar of the Classificatory Language." He formulated specific rules for the classificatory language of colon classification, as well as canons for the notational plane applicable to any classificatory language. He consolidated his experimental results and gave a model for analytico-synthetic classification schemes in the second edition of the Prolegomena to Library Classification (1957). The generalized facet formula for the analytico-synthetic scheme of classification has been incorporated in later editions of Colon Classification.

At the international level, the increased awareness and interest in classification research during this period may be gauged from the recommendation of the FID conference at Brussels in 1955. In this session the FID recommended that a deeper and more extensive study be made of the general theory of classification, including facet analysis and its application in the documentation of specific subjects.

The Classification Research Group in London started systematic research on faceted classification in 1952 and published its results in the Journal of Documentation and in ASLIB Proceedings. A Classification Research Study Group started functioning in the United States in 1958. The Dorking Conference in 1957 provided ample evidence of increased awareness of the need for continued research in classification. Dr. Ranganathan's continuing contact with FID/CA (Committee on General Theory of Classification) which was later replaced by FID/CR (Committee on Classification Research), and his active participation in classification research at the international level, stimulated research in this area, particularly in the depth classification need for retrieval of micro-thought, throughout the world. In 1964 at the Elsinore Conference Dr. Ranganathan outlined some of the classification problems to be pursued in these three planes (Idea, Verbal, and Notational). Towards the end of the same year, at the Rutgers Series on Systems for the Intellectual Organization of Information, Dr. Ranganathan reviewed the past and present investigations and the probable future lines of development of the colon classification. Both at the Elsinore conference and at the Rutgers Seminar, Dr. Ranganathan clearly brought out the differences between a mere faceted scheme and an analytico-synthetic scheme. The CC, in its four decades of development, has been continously attempting to make a closer approximation to the guided analytico-synthetic model. A. Neelameghan, in an article, "Analytico-synthetic Classification in Perspective," reviewed the design and development of the CC during the last forty years (1925-1965) and the Indian school of thought developed by Dr. Ranganathan and his associates.

Dr. Ranganathan moved to Bangalore in 1958 and established a Library Research Circle to continue his research activities on classificatory problems with the help of a small group of librarians. The activities of the center, however, could not be maintained on a continuing basis for lack of proper organization and financial support. The Documentation Research Centre, sponsored by the Indian Statistical Institute in Bangalore in 1962, is the first organized and adequately financed attempt to undertake programed research in library science in India. Since 1963, under the guidance of Dr. Ranganathan at the Documentation Research and Training Centre, compound subjects with a varying number of facets, all going with the same basic subjects, have been studied for more than a hundred basic subjects. The number of facets, presented by the compound subjects studied, has been found to vary from 2 to 30, with several characteristics being used in each facet. The research and experimental work at the DRTC led to a breakthrough across a long persistant barrier in the field of depth classification.

The methodology for the development of the colon classification is a very good illustration of the application of scientific method to research and development of classification. The design of the scheme of depth classification for specialized subject fields is entirely based on postulates, laws and principles. It provides a step by step procedure for the analysis of a subject, grouping the products on a helpful basis and allocating them to the various facets on the basis of fundamental categories.

The changes in the universe of subjects affect the evolution of classification. Systematic study of the attributes of the universe of subjects has been considered as the basis for research in classification by the Indian school of thought. As a result CC appears to have been endowed with sensitiveness to the changes in the universe of subjects and has been steadily improving its ability to meet the changing requirements of readers.

It is also being realized that the most productive method of meeting the challenges of classification of the dynamic universe of subjects is by building flexible methodology for the design of schemes of classification. Dr. Ranganathan and his assoicates, Neelameghan as well as others at the Documentation Research and Training Centre, are actively engaged in research and development in this area.

In 1963, Dr. Ranganathan developed a new methodology for the design of schemes for the classification of micro-subjects. His "Design of Depth Classification: Methodology," opened up considerable scope for applied and developmental research. It has resulted in formulation of empirical guiding principles for specific items of design work.

The new methodology developed has been applied since 1964. More than one hundred depth schedules for subjects in the fields of engineering, technology, and in other subjects, have been designed and are now being tested in specialized institutions and organizations. The splendid results of the postulational approach in designing these depth schedules has been reassuring.

Cataloging:

Along with research in the area of classification, Dr. Ranganathan carried on research on cataloging principles and has formulated the Classified Catalogue Code (CCC) based on extensive experimentation from 1926 to 1933 in the Madras University Library. The first edition of the Classified Catalogue Code appeared in 1934. The canons of cataloging formulated in 1938 are a landmark in cataloging research in India. These are the generalization of the empirical principles formulated earlier. Successive editions of the CCC have had adjustments to the empirical rules and the formulation of new ones. To meet the changes in the world of document production and the changing approaches of readers to information, successive blending of a priori and pragmatic research, together with applied and developmental research guided by the laws of library science, have been applied.

In 1945, along with the second edition of Classified Catalogue Code, Dr. Ranganathan published his Dictionary Catalogue Code. Five years later he brought out Library Catalogue: Fundamentals and Procedure (1950). He continued systematic studies on cataloging principles and codes and made a comparative study of the major cataloging codes of the world. He examined various codes, keeping in view his normative principles and his canons of cataloging, and published his findings in his book Headings and Canons, 1955.

Under the sponsorship of the UNESCO's Provisional International Committee on Bibliography and Documentation, Dr. Ranganathan investigated the problems connected with Asian Names-of-persons, and submitted his report in October 1953. The Documentation Sectional Committee of the Indian Standards Institution, on the basis of the findings of his report, formulated the "Indian standard practice for author treatment in the title page of a book" (IS: 793-1956).

Dr. Ranganathan recognized the symbiotic relation between classification and subject cataloging and on the basis of experimentation developed the chain procedure for deriving the name of subject of a document from the class number given to it. Rules for chain procedure also include the rules for rendering the names of subjects in class index entries. The findings from the extensive use of the chain procedure in large libraries, and in bibliographies such as British National Bibliography, plus the a priori research done, have established that the rules for chain procedure can be framed in alternative ways to procure the desired pattern of subject headings. The method of deriving "feature headings" from the class number by applying the chain procedure was incorporated into the fifth edition of the Classified Catalogue Code (1964). To improve upon the retrieval efficiency, several kinds of permutation of the terms in the "Heading of a Class Index Entry" are under experimentation at the Documentation Research and Training Centre.

The research program of the DRTC is primarily confined to the Indian school of thought developed by Dr. Ranganathan. The research staff are, however, fully aware of the potentiality of machine methods in information retrieval, and are now experimenting and developing software packages, using depth classification, for information retrieval.

In recent years a number of attempts have been made to formulate mathematical models of document retrieval systems based on information theory, mathematical logic and statistical methodology.

The training course in Documentation and Reprography at INSDOC since 1964 has created an atmosphere at INSDOC to carry out investigation and experimentation on classification and indexing, information retrieval techniques using both conventional methods and machine methods, and reprography techniques. The experimentation and research results are published in the Annals of Library Science and Documentation issued by INSDOC.

Though research facilities are very limited in India, the present generation of Indian librarians keeps in touch with present trends of research and development in library science and IR activities in Western countries, and they experiment with the newer thought within their own limited sphere. This, in fact, is one of the most encouraging features of Indian librarianship.

In earlier years of classification research Abgila (Annals and Bulletin of the Indian Library Association) and the Annals of Library Science published by INSDOC were the chief media for communication of work done in India. In recent years the Library Science with a slant to Documentation sponsored jointly by the Sarada Ranganathan Endowment for Library Science and the DRTC, the Annals of Library Science and Documentation sponsored by INSDOC, the Herald of Library Science, the IASLIC Bulletin, issued by the Indian Association of Special Libraries and Information Centres in India, the Library

Herald, published by the Delhi Library Association, and the Proceedings and Papers of the Annual Seminar of the DRTC, are the major periodicals recording Indian research activities.

Indian Standards

The national standards in India are prepared by the Indian Standards Institution (ISI). The ISI was set up in January 1947. The standards concerning documentation are prepared by the Documentation Sectional Committee (EC 2) of the ISI. Dr. Ranganathan who was Chairman of the EC 2 until 1967 was mainly responsible, through his writings and personal contacts, for stressing the importance of standardization in documentation.

The Documentation Sectional Committee has so far formulated the following Indian Standards for guidance of the Indian librarians.

IS: 18-1949	Abbreviation for the titles of periodicals.
IS: 382-1952	Practice for alphabetical arrangement.
IS: 790-1956	General structure of preliminary pages of a book.
IS: 791-1956	Half-title page of a book.
IS: 794-1956	Practice for table of contents.
IS: 795-1956	Canons for making abstracts.
IS: 1250-1958	Proof corrections for printers and authors.
IS: 1275-1958	Rules for making alphabetical indexes.
IS: 4-1963	Guide for layout of learned periodicals (rev.).
IS: 2381-1963	Recommendations for bibliographical reference.
IS: 2550-1963	Glossary of classification terms.
IS: 792-1964	Title-page and back of title-page of a book (rev.).
IS: 3130-1965	Code of practice for storage and use of micro-films of permanent value.
IS: 1358-1967	Practice for layout of catalog code (rev.).
IS: 796-1967	Glossary of cataloging terms (rev.).

Bibliographical References

Ranganathan, S. R. "Classification Research No Longer a Toddler" (Annals of Library Science 10(3 & 4):85-96, December, 1963).

_____ Freely Faceted Classification and Depth Classification. (Proceedings DRTC Seminar (4), 1966)

Indian Standards Institution Glossary of Classificatory Terms (IS: 2550-1963), 1963.

_____ Glossary of Cataloguing Terms (IS: 795-1967), 1967.

Ranganathan, S. R. "Library Classification Through a Century" (In Atherton Ed. Classification Research: Proceedings of the Second International Study Conference (Elsinore), 1964, p. 24).

___ Colon Classification (Rutgers series on systems for the Intellectural Organization of Information, 1965).

Neelameghan, A. "Analytico-synthetic Classification in Perspective." (Library Science with slant to Documentation 3(3):212-236, September 1966).

___ "Research on the Structure and Development of the Universe of Subjects" (Library Science with slant to Documentation 4(4): 336-355, December 1967).

Ranganathan, S. R. "Design of Depth Classification: Methodology" (Library Science with slant to Documentation 1(1):1-42, March 1964).

Neelameghan, A. and Gopinath, M. A. "Pragmatic Approach in the Design of a Depth Classification Schedule: A Case Study" (Library Science with slant to Documentation 2(1):55-68, March 1965).

___ "Research in Library Classification" (Library Science with slant to Documentation 4(4):356-381, December 1967).

Ranganathan, S. R. Chain Procedure: Its Development, Its Uses, Its Light on Basic Classes, and Its Problems (DRTC Seminar (3), Papers and Proceedings, 1965).

10. Role of Library Associations

Indian Library Association

Several state library associations--Andhra Pradesh Library Association (1914), Maharashtra Library Association (1921), Baroda Library Association (1924), Bengal Library Association (1925), Madras Library Association (1928), Punjab Library Association (1929)--are forerunners of the Indian Library Association, the national professional body established in 1933. The Association began with the following three objectives:

1. Furtherance of the library movement in India;
2. Promotion of the training of librarians; and
3. Improvement of the status of librarians.

In 1949, two new features--research in library science, and cooperation with the international organizations--were added and the Association redefined its objectives as follows:

1. Promotion of the library movement in India;
2. Promotion of the foundation of a trained class of librarians in India;
3. Promotion of research in library science;
4. Improvement of the studies and conditions of services of librarians; and
5. Cooperation with international organizations with similar objects.

Since its formation, the Indian Library Association has been holding biennial conferences to vitalize library activities in India and to bring about a common platform for all librarians. The subjects discussed at these conferences (cited below) and some of the major decisions made have brought about improved library service.

1933	Idiosyncracies in reading material
1937	Pitfalls in library administration
1940	Individuation in library science
1942	Reference service and reference books
1944	Library classification
1946	Library cataloging
1949	Library service in India
1951	Public library provision; Documentation problems
1953	Depth classification; Reference service and reference material

1956 Public library development in India; Bibliographical activities in India; School and children's libraries in India; Training for librarianship in India
1962 Bibliographical organization and control in India
1964 Model Public Libraries Bill; Provision of libraries in the fourth Five-Year Plan
1966 Development of school libraries during the fourth Five-Year Plan; Inter-library cooperation in India.

Though the all-India body created enthusiasm among all groups of librarians, its activities have remained mostly confined to the development and coordination of the general libraries, while also serving as a national link at the international level.

At the All-India Library Conference held at Nagpur in 1949, a group of librarians working in scientific organizations expressed their views about the necessity of forming a Special Libraries Association, since the Indian Library Association is mainly devoted to general library matters. However, the majority of the librarians failed to see any difference between this and the general library service and so the proposal was dropped.

To promote research and communication in library science, the Indian Library Association started a library journal, the Library Bulletin, in 1942, which changed its title to ABGILA (Annals, Bulletin and Granthalaya of ILA) in 1949, and to Journal of the Indian Library Association in 1955.

Indian Association of Special Libraries and Information Centres (IASLIC)

The attempt in 1949 to organize a special libraries association under the aegis of the Indian Library Association failed, but the situation changed rapidly and by 1955 the librarians working in special libraries, as well as the working scientists, strongly felt the need for such an organization. Several scientists and librarians in Calcutta resolved at a meeting on June 25, 1955, to organize the Indian Association of Special Libraries and Information Centres along the lines of ASLIB in England. The Association started functioning in September, 1955 with the following objectives:

(1) To encourage and promote the systematic acquisition, organization and dissemination of knowledge.

(2) To improve the quality of library and information services and documentation work.

(3) To coordinate the activities of and to foster mutual cooperation and assistance among the special libraries, scientific, technological and research institutions, learned societies, commercial organizations, industrial research establishments, as well as other information and documentation centres to the fullest extent.

(4) To serve as a field of active contact for libraries, information bureaus, documentation centres, scientists, research workers, specialists and others having common interest.

(5) To improve the technical efficiency of the workers in special libraries & information and documentation centres, and to look after their professional welfare.

(6) To act as a centre of research in special library and documentation techniques.

(7) To act as a centre of information in scientific, technical and other fields.

(8) To take all such action as may be incidental or conducive to the attainment of the objects of the Association, or any of them.

The functions of the Association can be grouped into six divisions as follows:

1. Documentation. This division provides bibliographic services on demand.

2. Education. This division organized foreign language classes for several years and is at present conducting one-year training courses in Special Librarianship and Documentation.

3. Publication and Publicity. This division issues the IASLIC Bulletin, the official organ of the Association since 1956, which contains articles mainly on special library methods and documentation techniques. The division is also responsible for organizing the conferences and seminars and publishing the reports on the proceedings for wider circulation.

4. Library and Information Service.

5. Library cooperation and coordination. This division fosters library cooperation and systematic interlibrary loans.

6. Documentary reproduction and translation. This division is entrusted with reprographic work and foreign language translation services. The work load for microfilm and photocopies, and translations is increasing each year.

It may be seen from its activities that the Association functions as a documentation center in the eastern region of India in addition to its other activities.

The Association has been holding seminars and conferences since 1956. The topics discussed at different sessions may give an idea of the problems which Indian scientists and librarians are trying to resolve.

1956   Mechanization of library services; Documentation problems in India.

1958   Industrial planning and information services; Training of special librarians in India.

1960   Development of libraries under the third Five-Year Plan (1961-1967); Rendering of Indic names; Bibliographical control of special libraries.

1961   Indic names.

1962(a) Methods of scientific communication; National Science Library for India; Centralization or decentralization of library and information services.

____(b) Users and library services; Education for librarianship in India.

1963   Document and data processing in special libraries in India; Problems and prospects of library associations in India.

1964   General vs. special classification schemes; Social Science documentation in India; Interlibrary loan and exchange of materials.

1965   Colon classification: a review of its use in India and abroad; Local documentation lists and their usefulness at the national level; Organization and responsibility of the library in academic and scientific institutions of India; Social Science research in India.

1966   Devaluation, its impact on libraries; Procurement of government documents and research reports.

1967   Indexing and abstracting services in India; Translation services.

IASLIC is the most dynamic library association in India and within its limited resources has contributed much to the improvement of special library services and documentation activities.

The Association is affiliated with both the International Federation of Library Associations (IFLA) and the Federation International de Documentation (FID).

The Indian Library Association (ILA) and the Indian Association of Special Librarians and Information Centres (IASLIC) are both working in close harmony to improve the library services in India. Unlike in many other countries, there is complete accord between these two national organizations.

It would be appropriate to mention here two seminars which were held in 1962 and covered the same issues. One was organized by the Indian Library Association and the other by the Indian Association of Special Libraries and Information Centres. The deliberations and decisions of these two seminars gave librarians a new outlook on the possibility of developing a network of library systems in India.

With the support of the government, the Indian Library Association held a seminar on "Bibliographical Organization and Control in India" held in Calcutta in February, 1962. The purpose of the seminar was to survey library resources in the fields of (a) science and technology, (b) the social sciences, and (c) the humanities, and then to suggest measures for the improvement of methods and techniques of organization and control. After discussing all aspects of organizational problems, a gathering of senior librarians recommended the following measures:

1. A large country like India with research materials scattered all over should have a decentralized and coordinated system of documentation and information services, based as far as practicable on the principle of subject specialization. The National Agencies specializing in particular subject fields should be entrusted with the task of documentation in the subjects of specialization.

2. The existing bibliographical ventures and documentation work already undertaken by different recognized agencies and specialized institutions, specializing in various subject fields, should be continued.

3. The seminar further recommended setting up of (a) permanent Policy Advisory Committee and (b) National Coordinating Body, and spelled out the broad functions of each.

The Policy Advisory Committee consisting of scientists, librarians, and documentalists should (i) advise the Government of India on matters relating to scientific information and encourage cooperative activity in the field of documentation in science and technology; (ii) stimulate research and experimentation of new techniques and methods in documentation and arrange periodic review.

The functions of the National Coordinating Body were laid down as follows:
- (a) to act as a repository for less used documents;
- (b) to compile bibliographical tools such as a Union Catalog of Periodicals;
- (c) to provide photo-copying facilities at regional centers and such other specialized centers having rich collections;
- (d) to provide translation facilities, in addition to those available in other centers;
- (e) to provide such information services as may be required to fill the existing gaps in various fields;
- (f) to act as a clearing house for information requirements; and
- (g) to foster and conduct research and development in methods, equipment and procedure.

Following this seminar, the Indian Association of Special Libraries and Information Centres held a second seminar at Dhanbad and recommended the following:

1. The advisability of a pyramidal structure of organization specializing in each subject field.

2. The acquisition policy of the proposed National Central Science Library should be such that, while avoiding unnecessary duplication, its holdings and those of the network of regional and other centers should be complete.

3. The setting up of a National Centre (a) to ensure that at least one copy of every book, report, periodical, etc., that might conceivably be required by the research workers is made available somewhere in the country, (b) to fill up gaps in special subject centers, (c) to act as a national repository for rarely used documents, and (d) to issue periodical lists of unlocated research documents.

The recommendations of the two seminars are similar and have given a definite line for the future development of the library system in India.

Other Professional Associations

Another all-India body, the Indian Academic Libraries Association, was organized in 1962. Its membership is open to academic librarians and to the teaching staffs of library schools. The academic libraries are the forerunners of the library movement in India, and as the majority of library personnel are employed in academic libraries, the Association should be able to accelerate its developmental activities. However, except for the organizational work at the beginning, very little has been achieved by this Association.

Besides the state library associations mentioned earlier, all the states, except Jammu and Kashmir, have state library associations. Bihar inaugurated its state library association in 1936, Assam in 1939, Kerala in 1942, Bombay and Orissa in 1944, Delhi and Gujarat in 1953, Hyderabad in 1954, Uttar Pradesh in 1956, Madhya Pradesh in 1957, and Mysore and Rajasthan in 1962.

These state library associations mostly confined their activities to the promotion of public libraries, the organization of training courses for the library staff at a semi-professional level, conferences, and publications. Some of the state associations are very active and primarily responsible for the State Library Act. It is unfortunate that the government has done very little to develop public libraries and only the Madras Library Association, the Andhra Library Association and the Mysore Library Association have succeeded in promoting legislation for establishing a network of public libraries in their respective states. Other state library associations are also trying hard to have legislation enacted in their states.

The state library associations, though mostly engaged in the promotional work of the public libraries, are the vital link and the most powerful force in the library movement in India. It is a pity, however, that each state association is functioning independently and in its own way, without attempting to coordinate its activities with those of the state associations in the other states. The All-India Library Association has not yet been able to function as a federal body to coordinate the activities in the different states.

Bibliographical References

Indian Association of Special Libraries and Information Centres. Annual Reports.

Indian Library Association. Annual Reports.

Kaula, P. N. "A Study of Library Organizations in India" (Herald of Library Science 3(2 & 3):130-148, 1964).

Part II: The U.S.A.

11. Prolegomena

In a brief memo in April, 1967, Dr. Ralph R. Shaw, Dean of Library Activities, University of Hawaii, invited me to come out from my routine activities in a special library and spend a few months observing current documentation activities in the United States. This was followed up by a formal communication from Dean Neal Harlow, Graduate School of Library Service, Rutgers University, confirming financial arrangements for three months' travel in the United States to observe current trends in documentation activities and to write a report on the basis of my experience.

This gave me an opportunity to revisit the country after sixteen years. (I was a student at the School of Library Service, Columbia University, in 1951.) In India, the information handling processes are manual and mostly handled in special libraries. I have described the special library and documentation activities in India in another part of this work. Except for doing work with a few experimental models, Indian librarians and documentalists have had very little practical experience with data processing equipment for information handling and other library activities. I went to the United States knowing very little about computer-based information systems, and I am not hesitant to add that I still know very little of the mechanics of machine methods. However, I accumulated a substantial volume of documents and references, which I tried to digest in order to get a clearer understanding of present trends and a projection of future computer-aided information retrieval activities and automated library services in the United States. My advisers at Rutgers scheduled my program of visits to different libraries and information centers, both in federal and non-federal bodies. They also put me in touch with several educators and experts engaged in teaching and research in library and information science.

During my three months' tour, I visited a number of fully or partly automated libraries and information centers attached to industry, information centers under the federal government, big research libraries including the Library of Congress and the John Crerar Library, private information centers managed commercially, and the developmental projects INTREX and TIP at the Massachusetts Institute of Technology. I had full opportunity to discuss several information transfer problems with the experts at these centers. Besides visits to different establishments, I had the opportunity to discuss educational and other related matters on information handling with Dr. Robert M. Hayes, Director of the Institute of Library Research, University of California; Dr. Don R. Swanson, Dean, Graduate Library School, University of Chicago; Dr. Jesse H. Shera, Mr. A. J. Goldwyn and Dr. Alan M. Rees, at the Center for Documentation and Communication Research, Western Reserve University; and Dean Neal Harlow and Dr. Susan Artandi at the School of Library Service, Rutgers University. Besides these academicians, I also had discussions with Mr. Forrest F. Carhart of the Library Technology Program, American Library Association; Mr. Karl E. Olsoni, Office of Scientific Information Service, National Science Foundation; Mr. Saul Herner and Mr. Melvin Weinstock of Herner and Company, a consulting and research firm in documentation. The primary contacts put me in touch with many other experts, but lack of space does not permit the mention of all their names. At my host university (School of Library Service, Rutgers University), I spent about six weeks reading literature on mechanized information retrieval and automated library service to get a clearer idea of current trends.

Normally, I had three broad queries regarding each of the centers I visited: how, for whom, and at what cost was the center established? At every center the management received me cordially and spent long hours with me (on occasion I might have bored them) explaining what they are doing and how. A description of the functions of these centers is given in the appendix.

For the second question, "for whom," the circulation statistics and the quantitative analysis of the data reached through feedback in the form of recipients' response provided the answer and also showed how effective the services are.

Prolegomena

Very little data on the cost question could be gathered either from publications or from other sources. The general conjecture, however, is that mechanization has made the library and information handling operations efficient and economical. As no records have as yet been provided to assess the comparative costs for automated and manual library procedures, the issue is still debated. Until operations in both manual and automated library systems are standardized to some extent and the functions are assessed quantitatively and qualitatively, any comparison of cost data would be incomplete and often misleading.

Paul J. Fasana has very correctly said that "Assessing costs of automation in libraries and trying to view them in a meaningful context is an extremely complicated procedure and at present there is no generally acceptable way of doing it."[1]

L. A. Schultheiss[2] computed the cost of manual operations of serials acquisition, cataloging, and circulation at the University of Chicago Library and came to the conclusion that the selection and acquisition of one book cost $4.85, the cataloging cost $8.67, and the circulation of each title cost $.41. This method for the analysis of cost, however, leaves much to be desired. Very few studies on the operational methods of cataloging have been made to bring about uniformity and standards; consequently the cataloging cost varies widely from library to library. While Schultheiss worked out $8.67 as the cost of cataloging a book, L. H. Linder[3] in 1965 determined that the average cost of cataloging a new book is $5.68 and that for each added copy is $1.42. Catherine Macquarie[4] gave the low figure of $1.76 on analyzing the cost in Southern California libraries. Because of this wide variation, such cost figures cannot be used confidently as a basis for comparing the manual and mechanized systems.

Henry Voos'[5] study, "On Standard Times for Certain Clerical Activities in Technical Processing" and other similar studies on different aspects of library operations offer some insight into standardized operations, production control, and cost analysis.

In libraries where the routine operations have been partly or fully automated, using either unit record data-processing equipment or the more sophisticated computer, the very common arguments in favor of such automation are that it reduces human error and that it is economical. No operational studies have yet been made to identify the nature or the percentage of human error in the manual methods of library operations and services. If it is accepted that the percentage of human error in the manual operations is significant, then the libraries in the United States, including the Library of Congress, the John Crerar Library, major university libraries, and others that have not mechanized routine operations are not only vulnerable on this count, but are also incurring losses due to such errors. Then, too, even in the mechanized operations several preliminary functions are intellectual and manual, and, therefore, equally subject to human error. The argument that automation has reduced or eliminated human error in library operations is more general than specific.

Very little data are available on the question of costs for many reasons. The libraries, small or medium, which provide automated library service or are planning to change over to a mechanized system have central computer facilities available in the organization. The mechanization, in most cases, is the result of encouragement from the computer people and is based on allotment of available computer hours. On the question of queuing problems, several librarians reported that the computer is allotted for the library work when it is not otherwise busy. It may not be too wrong to say that the availability of computer facilities has encouraged many small and medium-sized libraries to mechanize routine operations, and systems have been developed to utilize the available computer hours. In automated library service, very few studies have been made on operational systems to bring about uniformity and standards and to determine the cost correctly. Cost analysis is one area to which librarians have given very little attention. Automation may have affected the economic situation in the sense that it has released some manpower engaged in routine duties to attend to more intellectual functions, but, again, the evidence supporting this claim is limited.

The study of circulation control systems conducted by George Fry and Associates in 1960-61 indicated that the use of data processing equipment was a very expensive way to handle circulation control. In spite of this finding, following the report on the study of circulation systems that LTP published,[6] several major libraries changed over to mechanized systems.

In the process of mechanized serials control and cataloging, the single computer input produces a variety of lists as outputs by manipulation of the data. The bibliographic data and other information are fed into the computer in the process of acquisition; all the successive controls in the flow of serials, including book card, book label, etc., are obtained through manipulation of this initial input. Current awareness services and other library records are also produced by the manipulation of these data. At the Washington University School of Medicine Library, the computer-generated printed catalog is part of 17 lists obtained from the master tape. Computer-based cataloging is said to have reduced the clerical processes and to update these files by interpolating new records in sequence between old ones with less labor. An annual supplement is no solution since it increases the look-up points and repeated printing of cumulations will involve very substantial printing costs. In 1963, Linder[7] studied the cost of indexing 10,000 reports entered into an optical coincidence document storage system. The cost per document indexed under twelve to thirteen access points was $2.99. The cost of mechanized cataloging varies, depending on the system specifications and the machine used. The computer-generated microfilm catalog developed at the Technical Information Center of the Lockheed Missiles and Space Company is apparently much cheaper to produce than the computer-produced card catalog or the printed catalog in book form. It is not known yet how well readers will accept this new type of catalog. It is common in special libraries which have qualified literature searchers on their staffs for research scientists and technologists to delegate bibliographic searches to this group. The microfilm catalog may attain some degree of success in special libraries where independent searches are limited and open catalogs are not crowded by the readers as in academic and public libraries.

The computer with its power to manipulate, index, print, and update has liberated the catalog in any format (cards, printed page, or microfilm) from its former constraints. The computer-based on-line catalog, which the research group in Project INTREX is pursuing, holds great potentialities for direct man-machine interaction. The computer technology of the future may develop remote consoles at which users can converse interactively with the information systems, can formulate search problems in natural language, and can obtain meaningful results without much delay. But such technology still remains in the future.

The development and use of machine methods may gradually be changing the mode of library operations in some libraries, but what W. S. Buddington said at the SLA meeting in 1963 is still true. The key is "the word to think."[8] Present practice does not necessarily have to end with the catalog in an ash can and an IBM 7090 in its place; however, the advantage of radical suggestions is that we may well find better alternatives that are still short of computerization.

In 1964, Dr. Herman H. Fussler, Director of Libraries, University of Chicago, as Chairman of the Automation Committe of the Association of Research Libraries, pointed out that the library automation that has so far been developed has been worked out to improve the existing procedures rather than for experimentation with procedures reconstituted from the system point of view.

The increasing acceptance of the information center concept leads to the theory that information services will go beyond the librarian's traditional concept of reference services. The delineation of libraries and the information centers with regards to document and information handling services is somewhat artificial. It is always mentioned that the library and the technical information center are located in close proximity as the functions very often overlap and are interdependent. The library handles the conventional printed literature--books, journals, and other such printed material; the technical information center is given the responsibility of processing and storing the technical reports, memoranda, data files and other such research material which are generated by the scientists and technologists within the organization and outside. The technical information center analyzes and synthesizes the current scientific literature to provide the scientists current awareness bulletins and retrospective bibliographies and also organizes literature searches on demand. The establishment of technical information centers was a social necessity because the

Prolegomena

libraries had few facilities for organizing and disseminating the growing volume of scientific literature to meet the demand of scientists and other researchers. Scientific personnel with high academic qualifications and a deep knowledge of the subject came into the job as "literature searchers" or analysts--to scan, analyze, and review the scientific literature in preparation of authoritative bibliographic journals and reviews. The scientists and technologists interested in information transfer problems accepted the career of information scientists and began to assume responsibility for the storage and retrieval of scientific information and for using sophisticated hardware and software to mechanize the activities.

It is interesting to note that the gap between the library and the information center is narrowing as librarians assume more and more responsibility for serving the information requirements of scientific research. As far back as 1956, a few months after the decision of the International Congress of Libraries and Documentation Centers to create a new professional cadre as documentalists, Neal Harlow pointed out that the documentalists should be regarded as "we" not "they" and that the librarians "are likely to have the best training of all documentalists."[9]

Eugene Jackson, in 1961, predicted that "by 1980 it will be impossible to distinguish between special library service and documentation."[10] It may be that much before that time the special libraries will take up the information processing activities and will be responsible for seeing that all needed information promptly reaches the researchers who should have it and will also be responsible for the dissemination of internally produced information for wider use.

The John Crerar Library illustrates a typical case in which library service and information service have not been delienated as services in two separate areas. Several technical information centers will, however, continue to function as independent organizations to acquire, retrieve, and disseminate specialized information on different subjects covering world literature. The comprehensive bibliographic literature generated at these special information centers and the developed communication, facsimile reproduction, and transmission technology will allow the individual to gain easy access to any subject in world literature. Basic requirements for this information network are uniformity in procedure, and compatibility in formats, and, if not compatibility, easy convertibility from one system to another without high reprogramming costs.

I visited four technical information centers of which two are under federal government agencies, one in industry, and one in private enterprise. Of the two under federal bodies, the NASA Facility, under the National Aeronautics and Space Administration, is engaged in information retrieval activities to provide comprehensive access to the world's current literature on aerospace science and technology, and the MEDLARS system at the National Library of Medicine provides access to world literature on the biomedical sciences. In industry, the IBM Technical Information Retrieval Center (ITIRC) has been functioning since 1964 as the centralized information system to disseminate scientific and technical literature to the IBM community all over the world. The ITIRC system is linked to more than forty IBM libraries by teleprocessing techniques to make the retrieval service as effective and current as possible. The Institute of Scientific Information, one of the largest information centers, is engaged in the retrieval and dissemination of scientific literature on a commercial basis. The ISI provides a number of computer-based information services which include complicated bibliographic indexes, such as Index-Chemicus, Science Citation Index, and Permuterm Subject Index, and simpler services such as the current contents of different science journals. All the centers use computers and other associated equipment for the storage and retrieval of information and for printing bibliographic literature for current awareness and retrospective search services.

The input in the form of punched tape or cards is manipulated by the computer to produce indexes and other bibliographic literature and to provide literature search services, including the personalized selective dissemination of information (SDI) service. Computer-based operation has reduced processing and printing time lags. But mechanization itself, however well conceived and executed, is not enough. The intellectual part of the information processing such as scanning, analyzing, abstracting, and indexing under subject terms--in a word,

Prolegomena

all the pre-processes to feed the machine--must also be completed promptly, and there should be no backlog in encoding the literature if prompt service is to be provided.

Though the computer mechanism has reduced the processing and printing time, the time lag between the publishing date of the article in the primary journal and the date of its report in the current awareness bulletin is 3 to 18 months. This time lag may be due mainly to the delay in receiving the literature, assuming that there is no backlog in the intellectual processing to feed the machine. To minimize delay in the process of acquisition, all pertinent current literature, particularly from abroad, should be received by air mail and not be sea mail. This is an important matter and deserves consideration.

The desired results of computer processing and retrieval of information can be achieved only when similar attention is given to expediting the acquisition of literature and completing the intellectual part of the processing (processing for machine input) without time lag.

The information scientists and technologists attached to these centers are making continuous investigations on information processes with a view to improving the services through more refined methods and technology. For one wishing to get an idea of the effectiveness of the services provided by these centers, the data on circulation of the current awareness publications, the data on requests for demand bibliographies, and the response received from SDI notifications would be the major records for assessment. But simple statistical data may not always correctly reflect the use. Systematic user studies are more reliable to measure the performance of information activities, and there is a need for more such studies. There is an equal need to define the facilities more clearly to the scientific and technical community.

I was surprised to see the findings of the Denver Research Institute's (DRI) recent study on the channels of technology acquisition in commercial firms and the NASA dissemination program. The DRI study found that the various centers established for disseminating technological information are not widely used, in part because they are not readily accessible. The study concluded that "most individuals felt it too difficult to retrieve relevant materials from the mass of government publications and indicated that they expected to learn of important government developed technology through trade and professional channels."[11]

A similar study on the use of DDC (Defense Documentation Center) service presented almost the same findings. The Auerbach Report[12] revealed that 53 percent of the sample of DOD contractors and in-house engineers and scientists did not use the DDC Technical Abstract Bulletin (TAB). Of these, 21 percent were not aware of its existence.

Herner and Company[13] found essentially the same results in the Atomic Energy Commission when they studied the information gathering patterns of scientists and engineers engaged by AEC prime contractors.

On the use of MEDLARS tape, D. J. Urquhart, of the National Lending Library for Science and Technology, makes an interesting comment:

> ...there is nothing much a MEDLARS search can find which could not be found by using Index Medicus, although it might take longer to find it in Index Medicus. This is probably one of the reasons why the NLL is receiving so few requests for MEDLARS searches and why some of the requests we receive might be done more economically manually.[14]

Colonel Andrew A. Aines[15] has stressed the need for a series of studies to find out if self-supporting information activities are desirable, and he added that it seems quite probable that in the future there will be more dependence on the market place as a determinant of success.

The information centers are still in evolutionary forms. Experimentation on size, scope, mechanization, and level of service will continue until some uniformity in the information systems is reached. Test methodology to establish the comparative performance of systems and costs is still in an experimental stage. The Comparative Systems Laboratory at Western Reserve University is currently carrying out experiments to identify the elements necessary for conducting reliable experiments in the testing of retrieval systems. Hopefully, a testing methodology will develop from these experiments. A very interesting model incorporating basic components of retrieval systems has been formulated and experimentally tested in the laboratory. The experiment included, among others, the identification, enumeration, and verification of factors operating within individual components. The cost data on existing information systems are incomplete and often unreliable. M. E. Stevens,[16] in his state-of-the-art report on automatic indexing, has pointed out the lack of objective data on costs of indexing. Melvin Weinstock[17] records that within the government's information systems, there are 36 different library classification systems, 31 different cataloging systems, 45 unique index vocabularies or thesauri, and 21 different computer format and coding systems, each incompatible with any other system within the government. As standardization in techniques and forms is a prerequisite for the emergence of a network of libraries, information centers and switching centers, researches aimed at developing compatibility in the areas of equipment, systems, codes, and thesauri are now going on. Continual improvement in machine design and capability and marketing of new equipment may hinder desired progress in this direction.

In the United States, the growth of scientific literature appears to parallel the growth of scientific research and it is growing at the rate of 12 percent a year.

We all know that it is becoming increasingly difficult for an individual to keep up with current literature, even in the narrowest field of specialization. As the rate at which a reader can read and absorb information remains relatively constant, within the next eight years his ability to cover the literature in his field of specialization will be reduced by one-half. This means either he will have to confine himself to more selective readings or he will have to specialize in a still narrower area, which will, in turn, lead to a further narrowing of the subjects and areas of specialization. To process double the present volume of literature, either the machine capabilities will have to be improved or the present computer time will have to be doubled. This is simple arithmetic, but the future literature may be more complex as well as bulkier. This is the crux of the information problem. To retrieve and disseminate this increased volume of scientific information, the computers will solve many of the problems, but not all. In the future, researches on information storage and retrieval modes for selectivity of the literature may become more important than finding methods for total coverage. Garfield's Citation Index, Kessler's "Bibliographic Coupling" and his experimental design of the Project TIP, studies by J. W. Tukey,[18] N. M. Kessler,[19] and Derek de Solla Price[20] on the statistical characteristics of networks of cited and citing scientific papers to determine the family matrix of the journals, and other similar researches, will have a far-reaching impact on future information retrieval.

The use of the computer and associate equipment--the common element in many of the libraries and information services that I have mentioned--is the most significant development in information handling activities in the last decade. An equally significant development is the entrance into the field of information services of scientific personnel with high academic qualifications and with a broad knowledge of the different areas of science and technology. Senior scientists and technologists whose broad knowledge is well known by research scientists and management are now working in libraries and information divisions handling more difficult information requests, conducting comprehensive and critical searches according to the specifications of the inquirer, compiling bibliographies and continually reviewing scientific literature in specified fields of interest.

Further, their knowledge of the subject is helpful in maintaining close liaison with the scientists and technologists engaged in research and in keeping up with their research activities. This creates effective communication between the library and information people and the users, which is always necessary for dynamic library service and for evaluating its effectiveness.

In the Smith, Kline and French Laboratories (SK&F) an ideal situation has been reached. The scientific people attached to the Science Information Division assist the research team on any company project and contribute at each stage of the research and development process. All through the processes they are responsible for supplying

Prolegomena

information, interpreting it, and evaluating it; and even after marketing, they continue to be responsible for answering questions from scientists and physicians about any particular drug, its effects and how it acts. The science information people at the SK&F laboratories not only help the research scientists with needed information, but act as equal partners in the research team.

For the problem of disseminating the growing scientific information, there is no panacea to be found in a moratorium on publications, in documentary metamorphosis, or in automation. The tools and methods to be used for the selection and retrieval of literature must be diverse and must be applicable to varied conditions. Machine or manual, the aid must be made more specific, with finer subject arrangement and more detailed indexing, in order that the search amidst the increasing mass of recorded information may be narrowed down. Human judgment is the most critical element in the retrieval process and this is one factor which will make or break any information handling system.

When we were just entering the computer age Norbert Wiener said:

> That we shall have to change many details of our mode of life in the fact of the new machines is certain; but these machines are secondary, in all matters of value that concern us, to the proper evaluation of human beings for their own sake and to their employment as human beings, and not as second-rate surrogates for possible machines of the future. [21]

In the following chapters, I shall review the trends in documentation activities and in the appendix I shall describe the establishments and projects I saw.

Bibliographical References

1 Fasana, Paul J. "Determining the Cost of Library Automation" (ALA Bulletin, June 1967, p. 656-661).

2 Schultheiss, L. A. Advanced Data Processing in the University Library. New York, Scarecrow Press, 1962.

3 Linder, L. H. "Comparative Costs of Document Indexing and Book Cataloging" (Special Libraries 56(10):724-726, December, 1965).

4 Macquarie, Catherine "Cost Survey: Cost of Ordering, Cataloging,

and Preparations in Southern California Libraries." Library Resources and Technical Services, Fall, 1962, p. 337-50.

5 Voos, Henry Standard Times for Certain Clerical Activities in Technical Processing. Doctoral thesis. Rutgers University, New Brunswick, 1964.

6 American Library Association The Use of Data Processing Equipment in Circulation Control, Library Technology Reports, Circulation Systems. Chicago, The Association, July, 1965.

7 Linder, L. H. "Indexing Cost for 10,000 Documents," in Automation and Scientific Communication. American Documentation Institute, 26th Annual Meeting, 1963. Papers, vol. 2. Washington, D. C., ADI, 1963, p. 147-148.

8 Buddington, William S. "The Word to Think" (Special Librarian 55(8):564-568, October, 1964).

9 Harlow, Neal "Documentation and the Librarian" (Library Journal 81:1083-1085, May, 1956).

10 Jackson, Eugene B. "Special Libraries" (Library Trends 10:209-23, October, 1961).

11 Greenberg, D. S. "Civilian Technology: NASA Study Finds Little 'Spin-Off' " (Science 157(3792):1016, September 1, 1967).

12 Auerbach Corporation, Department of Defense. User Study, Phase I, Final Technical Report, 1151-TR3, to the Advanced Research Projects Agency, Philadelphia, May, 1965.

13 Herner and Company. The Use of Atomic Energy Commission Technical Information Tools and Services. Report to the U. S. Atomic Energy Commission, The Company, Washington, D. C., February, 1962.

14 Urquhart, D. J. "Developing User Independence" (ASLIB Proceedings 18(12):351-356, December, 1966).

15 Aines, Andrew A. "Science, Technology, and the Library" (Special Libraries 57(1):15-20, January, 1966).

16 Stevens, M. E. Automatic Indexing: A state-of-the-art report. (National Bureau of Standards Monograph 91) Washington, D. C., Government Printing Office, 1965, p. 153.

17 Weinstock, Melvin "Network Concepts in Scientific and Technical Libraries" (Special Libraries 58:328-334, May-June, 1967).

18 Tukey, J. W. The Citation Index and the Information Problem. Princeton University, Statistical Techniques Research Group, 1962.

19 Kessler, N. M. Some Statistical Properties of Citation in the Literature of Physics.

20 Price, D. J. de Solla "Is Technology Historically Independent of Science?" Paper presented at a symposium on the Historical Relations of Science and Technology, Montreal, December, 1964.

21 Wiener, Norbert The Human Use of the Human Beings; Cybernetics and society. Boston, Houghton Mifflin, 1950, p. 2.

12. Special Libraries and Technical Information Centers

In the United States, the nineteenth century saw the beginning of public library service and with the twentieth century, a new type of library--the "special library"--began to serve readers in special subject areas. It would thus meet the need of business and professional men, public administrators, manufacturers, and scientists. Early in this century, John Cotton Dana, the prime mover for a special libraries association in the United States, recognized the special library as the best answer to the needs of specialized groups. He defined the special librarian as "the modern man of affairs." With a view to uniting on a national basis all the libraries attached to special departments and devoted to special subject fields, he formally proposed the establishment of the Special Libraries Association in July, 1909. Dana admitted the lack of inclusiveness in his definition of special library and pointed out that special libraries are so varied in their character and in the use made of them that no definition would satisfactorily include all of them. Even during this early period of development, Dana and several other pioneers spoke about the possibilities of special services, the development of library systems, and the coordination of libraries and information clearing houses. It is easy to identify these early ideas with some very modern developments in documentation that are based upon similar clearing houses and coordinated activities, now called the "network concept."

The first directory of special libraries, which appeared in the second issue of <u>Special Libraries</u> in April, 1910, recorded a list of nearly one hundred such libraries in the United States.

Otlet used the word "documentation" in 1907 (two years prior to Dana's move for special libraries in the United States) when he needed a term to cover the activities both in libraries and in archives. He called the international congress held in Brussels in 1910 the "Congress de bibliographie et de documentation," thus combining two words which had different meanings and were mutually exclusive.

The Association of Special Libraries and Information Bureaux (ASLIB), founded in England in 1924 with the same purpose avoided use of the word "documentation." The word became significant and its meaning became broader when the Institut International de Bibliographie, founded in 1895, changed its name to Institut International de Documentation in 1931. The Institut subsequently acquired a federative character, consisting of national and international members, and changed its name to International Federation for Documentation (FID) in 1938.

Between 1907 and 1931, the word "documentation" was used with a variety of shades of meaning and commonly indicated, in a stricter sense, the methods and means for making the scientific contents of a document accessible to the user. The American Documentation Institute came into existence in 1937 and the Centre National de la Recherche Scientifique (CNRS) was established in France, in 1939, for the organization and dissemination of special knowledge. In 1939, Jean Gerard provided a broad difinition of the word "documentation." This became the FID definition: as the creation, transmission, collection, classification, and use of documents, documents being broadly defined as recorded knowledge in any format. The whole gamut of operations, from the creation of new knowledge to its arrival at the user, is covered in documentation through the processes of report writing, publication, abstracting, classification, indexing, reassembly, presentation, and dissemination.

The needs created by intensive scientific research during and after the second world war period saw the emergence of the documentalist as an independent entity. As the fields of scientific investigation became more and more complex, the need for information from related disciplines became greater. Expansion of scientific library and documentation services to integrate scientific and technical information and bibliographic work with the different stages of activity in scientific research and experimental design, was accepted as essential to developments in science, technology and industry.

The Brussels session of the International Congress of Libraries and Documentation Centres, in 1955, considered the existing rigid methods of library management inadequate to cope with modern standards of development in scientific research and the librarians not capable of developing and perfecting the necessary forms and methods of scientific and technical information and bibliography. The assembly stressed the need for separate professional cadre for documentation activities.

Though several active groups began working on the development of a sound program to discover the needs of the various users of documentation, the entire field of documentation remained in a somewhat chaotic state, partly due to the failure of the profession to define precisely what documentation is, what the relationship between librarianship and documentation is, and what kind of training the documentalist needs. The recruitment for documentation work remained to be drawn from subject specialists or personnel trained in library science.

Ralph Shaw[1] looked upon documentation as a complete cycle system of providing information. Jesse Shera[2] defined it as that aspect of librarianship concerned with the organization and dissemination of graphic records for their most efficient use within and among groups of scientists, to the end that they will receive, in a manner as effective as possible, the data and other information that they require for the promotion of their work.

Since Dana defined the special library in 1909 as a dynamic organization, the objectives of special libraries have changed with the growth and complexity of literature and the changed pattern of users' demands. During the last sixty years several librarians and other authorities have identified the changes and redefined the objectives and activities which come under the purview of special libraries under more modern conditions. The October, 1952 issue of <u>Library Trends</u> summarized the trend of special libraries, and several authors including Herman Henkle, the editor, defined special librarianship in terms of services. Henkle says, "The primary characteristic of special librarianship is not so much the subject content of the collection or the type of organization in which the library is operating, or the particular personnel it serves, but rather the kind of service it gives."[3] Shaw[4] stressed the fact that the broad objective of special libraries is to provide information needed, when needed, and in

Information Centers

the form in which it is needed.

In 1963, Susan Artandi[5] reviewed the objectives of special librarianship, as laid down by different library experts in the last decade in order to correlate current thinking with future trends in special library service. It is evident from recent trends in special library activities that the wide gap between the knowledge brought in by the special librarian and that required from the viewpoint of the documentation activities which existed in the 1940's and 1950's, is narrowing as librarians are becoming more and more conscious of their responsibility to transmit information to users in the needed form. Allen Kent very correctly said, "As far as functions of special libraries are concerned they coincide completely or partially with those of documentation, depending on how narrowly or broadly a particular librarian or documentalist views his field."[6]

In September, 1964, the Professional Standards Committee of the SLA, after several years of hard labor, formulated objectives and standards for special libraries, which also include the characteristics and performance of the presently developing information centers. As in the case of all standards, the Committee's document needs periodic review and reassessment to serve as a guideline for the development and attainment of high quality library and information service.

However, the scope and methods of the special library, as a dynamic organization oriented to service, have continued to change with time and with scientific and technological progress, and the question of what special librarianship is, is still as difficult to answer as before.

The magnitude of information problems in science and technology in the age of space research and nuclear research, and the opportunities to apply new information transfer technologies led to the establishment of newer types of organizations, called technical information centers, in the late 1950's, to meet the challenging problems in retrieving and transferring information. The information centers encompass a broader spectrum of information activities than originally thought to be covered by library service. The rapid proliferation of such centers in the field of science and technology, both in industry and in federal bodies, is in recognition of the need for establishments to furnish users with processed information in an assimilable form with an explicit relationship to their research interests. The full spectrum of science information activities as envisaged by information centers is found to be more complex than the librarians have so far been expected to solve.

Simpson has defined the scientific information center in the following way:

> A scientific information center exists for the primary purpose of preparing authoritative, timely and specialized reports of the evaluative, analytical monographic or state-of-the-art type. It is an organization staffed in part with scientists and engineers and, to provide a basis for its primary function, it conducts a selective data and information acquisition for processing program. [7]

Alan Rees defines the information center by its functions: "selected, specific and synthesized information derived from a preselected store of documents."[8]

In his report Science, Government and Information, Alvin Weinberg has urged the establishment of more and better specialized information centers. He states:

> We believe that the specialized information center, backed by large central depositories, might well become a dominant means to the transfer of technical information.... Specialized information centers, to be fully effective, must be operated in closest possible contact with working scientists and engineers in the field. The activities of the most successful centers are an intrinsic part of science and technology. The centers not only disseminate and retrieve information; they create new information.... [9]

It may be inferred from these definitions and recommendations that the information center and the library are separate entities in the process of scientific communication. The former is charged with responsibility for evaluating, interpreting, and analyzing information and data while the latter offers unevaluated and unprocessed documents or document references or both. Both are, however, not only complementary but very often their functions and purposes overlap.

Simpson, an exponent of the information center concept, conceded that conventional library systems were adequate up to the twentieth century; special libraries then developed to provide specialists more specific information not available through general libraries. Specialized information centers are but an extension of that trend.

There is, however, an increasing awareness of the role of special librarians in the total information transfer chain and many special libraries furnish selected information and thereby approximate the services of information centers.

Weinberg's report drew a mixed reaction from librarians. Shaw, in an article in Science, pointed out that "we are equating improvement with change and emphasizing the means rather than the end."[10] He called for a careful and detailed study of "search strategy" and of the various methods of handling information. A computer that can answer questions "is not a miracle;" it is one of many modern methods of processing information. The Weinberg Report can become a most important document if it opens the eyes of the government, the administrators, and the librarians to the most efficient methods for handling the information explosion.

The encouraging congressional hearings and reports by various presidential committees, liberal federal grants, and the developing computer technology for processing, communicating, and disseminating information initiated the establishment of several hundreds of specialized information centers in the United States in the last decade. Many of these special centers have been established to serve contractors on government research and development activities; and many of these are attached to industrial establishments to feed these industries with needed information. The subject coverage of some of these information centers is broad while others may cover only a particular branch of science and technology.

A variety of data processing equipment is used for storage and retrieval systems to produce a variety of bibliographic services such as announcement bulletins, indexes, abstracts, and citation references in printed form as well as personalized services such as the selective dissemination of information (SDI). Some of these information centers not only identify but also supply documents either in printed or in microform.

These specialized information centers are normally headed by scientists and technologists (with or without a formal education in library science) who are now commonly known as information scientists. To make the services economical and, at the same time, more effective from the users' point of view, these information scientists make continuous studies on "search strategy" and on improved methods of mechanization.

Present day activities of most information centers are still limited to the retrieval and dissemination of information (perhaps more correctly expressed as "document retrieval"). Very few centers have gone a step further to synthesize information or data from published and unpublished sources to create new information pertinent to the individual request.

There are several large information centers under the federal system. The Defense Documentation Center (DDC) in the Department of Defense is for the administration of its scientific and technical information or STINFO. The Atomic Energy Commission (AEC) has developed a mechanized information processing system to supply scientific and technological data in nuclear science to government agencies, medical and scientific groups working in universities and other research establishments, and industry. At the National Library of Medicine MEDLARS, a computer-based system is operating for the dissemination of world medical literature. The National Aeronautics and Space Administration (NASA) has developed dynamic information services for scientists working in the aerospace area.

The Office of Technical Services (OTS) under the U.S. Department of Commerce (lately renamed Clearinghouse for Federal, Scientific, and Technical Information (CFSTI) which is the center in the federal government for the collection, control, and dissemination of government research reports and translated scientific and technical literature, has been placed under the National Bureau of Standards. The federal information system is now attempting to coordinate and formalize the information-producing and information-using agencies by designating the area of responsibility for these agencies, and by designating the Committee on Scientific and Technical Information (COSATI) as the coordinating body.

The technical information centers of industrial establishments

Information Centers

also have dynamic information retrieval and dissemination systems to support company research. These information centers are encouraged to mechanize information retrieval, if computer facilities are available.

During the last few years a number of private firms have begun to provide literature search and bibliographic and consulting services on a commercial basis. Some of these firms specialize in procuring library materials, centralized cataloging, foreign language translation, publishing indexes, abstracts or current awareness bulletins, and SDI services. In 1962, the Special Libraries Association compiled and published a descriptive list[11] of these organizations for the benefit of those who want to subscribe to such services.

Competition prevails among the commercial enterprises in marketing efficient information services; this competition may in the future help to develop the criteria for measuring the performance of information activities and the costs of such services.

The Government Information Services Committee of the Special Libraries Association is functioning to keep users informed of the newer services and trends in government supported information agencies and to make the agencies aware of the constantly changing needs of users. To determine the opinions of users on the dissemination of government contract generated information, in 1965 the Committee made a survey among 100 librarians from the government, universities, and industry, since the librarian-users are the focal point of information service in a user organization and also since the librarian-user speaks knowledgeably about the use made by the scientists and technologists in the organization. Such a survey provides feedback and guidance to the government information agencies.[12]

There is no updated data on the special libraries and information centers in the United States. The National Science Foundation's directory of specialized science information services recorded 427 information centers in the United States in November, 1961.

Dr. Anthony T. Kruzas,[13] in his statistical report on special library resources in the United States, which was based on data collected in 1961 and 1962, listed 2,202 college and university libraries, 2,163 company libraries, 1,221 government agency libraries,

2,560 libraries operated by other organizations, and 387 public libraries--a total of 8,533 special libraries and information centers in the United States.

It is estimated that about 10,000 special libraries and information centers are now operating in the United States.

Bibliographical References

1. Shaw, Ralph R. "Documentation: complete cycle of information service" (College and Research Libraries 18:452-54, November, 1957).

2. Shera, Jesse H. "Research and Development in Documentation" (Library Trends 10:224-42, October, 1961).

3. Henkle, Herman H. Letter dated June 19, 1952. (Library Trends 1:208, October, 1952.)

4. Shaw, Ralph R. "Documentation: complete cycle of Information Service" (College and Research Libraries 18:452-54, November, 1957).

5. Artandi, Susan "Special Library Services: current thinking and future trends" (Special Libraries 54:103-106, February, 1963).

6. Kent, Allen "Documentation" (Library Trends 10:224-42, October, 1961).

7. Simpson, G.S. "Scientific Information Centers in the United States" (American Documentation 13(1):43-57, January, 1962).

8. Rees, A.M. "Librarians and Information Centers" (College and Research Libraries 25(3):200-204, May, 1964).

9. Weinberg, A.M. Science, Government and Information, 1963.

10. Shaw, Ralph R. "Information Retrieval" (Science 140:606-9, May 10, 1963).

11. "A Survey of Commercial Library Services" (Special Libraries 54(5):263-270, May-June, 1963).

12. SLA Government Information Services Committee "Users Look at Information Centers" (Special Libraries 57:45-50, January, 1966).

13. Kruzas, Anthony T. Special Libraries and Information Centers: A statistical report on special library resources in the U.S. Detroit, Gale Research, 1965.

13. Libraries and Machines

Jesse H. Shera[1] in a recent article "Librarians Against Machine" mentioned the slower rate in environmental changes for automated information retrieval and accused the professional librarian of being orthodox and skeptical about adopting the newer computer technology for information handling and library service.

The attitude of earlier librarians towards the use of machines, however, presents a somewhat different picture. From the very beginning, librarians recognized the need for improved techniques for information processing and servicing and, wherever possible, they experimented with the application of technology to improve library service. The use of the typewriter as a possible tool for cataloging was mentioned as early as 1877 at the New York Conference of Librarians. H. Taylor,[2] in 1915, invented the perforated stencils which have more recently been called "peek-a-boo" cards. In 1920, H. E. Soper[3] invented a mechanism for information retrieval which was an improvement on Taylor's perforated stencils. E. Goldberg,[4] in 1931, patented one of the earliest devices for scanning and selecting from film strip and photograph copying. In 1936, Ralph Parker[5] experimented with the application of Hollerith cards to circulation systems at the University of Texas. The circulation system of the Montclair Public Library introduced the Hollerith punch card machine in 1941.[6] The University of Florida also experimented with a mechanized circulation system at about the same time.[7]

During the late 1940's, technological advancement brought to market more sophisticated Hollerith and other unit record machines for sorting and reproducing. Though these machines were not primarily designed for bibliographical purposes, some of the librarians and documentalists began to experiment with the application of data processing equipment to handle library operations.

The first successful application of punch cards in printing book catalogs was made in 1951 at King County (Washington) Public Library.

In 1956, two other catalogs were printed using punched card methods.[8] Parker made the first extensive application of punched card methods to library routines at the University of Missouri Library in 1957.

Davis and Draeger[9] investigated the feasibility of a microfilm scanner, using decimal coding, sometime in 1935. The results of this investigation helped Vannevar Bush to build a prototype machine in 1938-39, which combined a microfilm record of documents with an indexing code along the edge of the film. In July, 1945, Bush's article[10] "As We May Think" predicted that photographic and electronic techniques could be combined for literature searching. In 1946-47, Shaw, then Librarian at the U.S. Department of Agriculture Library, made many changes by modifying Bush's electronic approach to meet bibliographic requirements and designing a new machine which he called the "Rapid Selector." The Rapid Selector could search a 2,000 foot reel of 35 mm roll film by the use of optically coded binary patterns that identified each document image on the film frame. Shaw's Rapid Selector went through significant remodeling at Yale University and at the National Bureau of Standards to simplify and improve its operating systems. The U.S. Navy, Bureau of Ships, installed a more improved model of the Rapid Selector for retrieving correspondence. This machine was developed by FMA, now a division of Cutler-Hammer, Inc.

Shaw,[11] using phototechnology, designed a prototype machine, the "Photoclerk," and put it into operation at the Department of Agriculture Library in July, 1948. After two years of experimentation in his library, Shaw carried out experiments on the use of photography for clerical routines in several cooperating libraries and made a comparative cost analysis of photoclerical processes against manual operations. The machine was produced and marketed by Remington Rand, Library Bureau Division.

H. Peter Luhn, in 1947, set up one of the first mechanized retrieval systems in which punch cards were read and sorted by an IBM machine called the "Luhn Scanner." Later, Luhn devised a computer program to handle "auto-abstracting." Luhn also developed the program of disseminating information selectively to individuals in accordance with an "interest profile" with the help of a machine. Luhn called it a "business intelligence system."

The Livermore Laboratories in California developed a prototype IBM device, which was a combination of electronic and photographic media using electronic beams to produce micro-images. In the early fifties, Kodak developed "Minicard" and with it demonstrated that a document could be filed under as many headings as necessary. The search could be limited to selected portions of the total file and the machine would make extra copies of each minicard master to be filed under as many subject headings as desired.

Hand, Moore, and Runge,[12] in 1951, wrote an interesting article, "The Special Library of the Future," in which they projected the developments in management of a special library in 1975. In this article, the authors predicted that libraries would not maintain back numbers of periodicals; all items of more than one year old would be microfilmed and filed for use. The libraries would be provided with microfilm cameras for reproduction; "wire recorders" for recording the proceedings of the meetings; television and facsimile transmitters to transmit the needed information; and punched card systems for control of circulation and other routine operations in the library. The authors also thought of a card catalog setup with dial access. The dialing would release all the cards on a particular subject for scanning and then refile them when no longer needed. The authors contended that all these automatic machines and push button systems would release the professional librarians from routine and repetitive tasks, allowing them to attend to intellectual operations. The enthusiastic authors projected the automation in libraries based on their knowledge of technology and the machines developed during that time. They failed to see that with successive developments in technology many newer and more sophisticated machines would come within 25 years. The punched card data processing equipment which they thought would be used for routine operations in libraries began to be replaced by electronic computers and more sophisticated machines within 10 years. This article may simply amuse the present generation of librarians and other thinkers of automated libraries, but I have especially mentioned it here since this may be equally true for all such future projections of automation programs, particularly when technology is developing at a rate faster than ever before. The rational organization of the transfer and utilization of information calls for the application of up-to-date technical means and their constant improvement.

Shaw, in his Windsor Lecture in March, 1950, surveyed both the existing and developing machines which excited some of the librarians as a probable solution to bibliographical control of increased literature output and summed up his findings as follows:

> Use of machines for bibliographical purposes is developing, and it is developing rapidly, but the use of machines for more efficient management of literature and of the intellectual content of literature calls for a great deal of information which is not now available. [13]

In the 1950's, the manufacturers of computers and other data processing equipment for handling bookkeeping and accounting data began to cover a much broader spectrum and increased their research in the information area in order to gain technological superiority in processing, communicating, and disseminating technical information. Enthusiasm for research work and experimental design on mechanized information retrieval also speeded up during the late 1950's when the federal government and other sources began to provide support for the exploitation of automated information retrieval. The increased research on hardware and software achieved some degree of success on machine capabilities for information handling, but many major problems remained unsolved.

The International Conference on Scientific Information held in November, 1958 in Washington recorded that during the past ten years there had been numerous attempts to use machines for handling information problems but that many of these had failed because fundamental problems remained unsolved. The committee of experts also pointed out that many machine proponents had made claims for systems of information handling which could not be substantiated from an economic point of view or, in fact, from the standpoint of technical feasibility.

In an article in 1960, Calvin N. Mooers traced the development of retrieval machines and remarked:

> Although during the past twenty years (since the date of Bush's machine) there have been attempts to build high-speed selecting machines for information retrieval, at the present time I think that it cannot honestly be said that we have done too well. We do not have a machine which is an altogether happy answer to the problems of search and selection...[14]

More technological development in machine retrieval made it quite apparent that the machine can retrieve nothing that has not been properly indexed or coded in the first place. This led an able group of researchers to experiment and develop indexing and retrieval theory. The three major innovations in indexing methods in the late 1950's were the "Uniterm" concept of Mortimer Taube, the "Descriptor" system of Calvin Mooers, and the "Role Indicator" method of Western Reserve University.

Taube's "Uniterms" are simply the significant terms, or key words in documents. In Calvin Mooers' "Descriptor," the terms are derived by analyzing a collection of related documents on a subject. The terms are then listed in a dictionary form or thesaurus together with all their synonyms. The "Role Indicator" of the Western Reserve system shows the relationships between the terms used.

Since 1955, the Western Reserve system has been used to index and abstract the world's metallurgical literature. The work is handled by a prototype high speed electronic machine called a "Search Selector" (the G. E. 250). Taube's "Uniterm" is used, among others, by a number of government agencies. With federal and non-federal financial support, research continues in an attempt to systematize the world's total output of scientific and technical literature.

Librarians and information scientists are working harder and experimenting on indexing methods, mechanized information processing, and automated library service. The technological development of automatic data processing equipment has brought varying degrees of success during recent years and has provided remedies for some of the complex problems in information handling, but have by no means solved all the problems.

> The real difficulty in devising mechanized systems for organizing and searching large collections of scientific information is not technological; it is intellectual. The storage

of information is not the key problem. The difficulty is how to organize the information for effective retrieval.[15]

Ben-Ami Lipetz has lately written in Scientific American:

> The difficulty of handling analytical problems has so far limited the use of mechanical techniques in information storage and retrieval work to applications that never required much analytical judgment on the part of the humans who formerly did the work.... There is great need for machines to take over significant portions of intellectual work. Faster, larger, cheaper computers are not the complete answer, although they will be certainly necessary.[16]

The computers available at industrial and other research establishments, however, continue to encourage the big and small libraries attached to these centers to experiment and to adopt fully or partly automated library services. These services include mechanization of circulation control; serials control (renewals, check in, routing slips, and binding records); control of book orders; processing work, including accession lists, announcement bulletins and production of card and book catalogs; as well as retrospective searches and current awareness service.

It is now established beyond doubt that electronic equipment can handle such functions as ordering, cataloging, and circulation and serials control with great speed and accuracy, either as separate operations or as part of total systems as in the IBM Advanced Systems Development Division Library at Los Gatos. The economics of reorienting the routine library operations from the conventional to the non-conventional computerized system and its efficiency in day to day operations depend on many factors including the allotment of computer hours by the host organization, the size of the library collection, and the nature of services provided. In some of the libraries experiments are being conducted on an individual module basis for measuring the efficiency of the mechanization of different operations in a library.

A study of circulation control systems conducted by George Fry and Associates in 1960-61, however, indicated that the use of data processing equipment was a very expensive way to handle circulation control. Despite this fact, following the report of the study (published by Library Technology Reports[17]), several libraries continued the installation of data processing equipment for this purpose. George Fry and Associates[18] then studied the installations at the Widener Memorial Library at Harvard University; the University Research Library, University of California; and the Research Library at the Thomas J. Watson Research Center of IBM to find out the utilization of each system in its most efficient form and the present cost, and to draw conclusions as to the reasons why each operation was developed and installed. The report provides a guideline to those who contemplate automating the circulation system and who wish to know about costs.

Experiments and operational research continue, at several centers, to attempt to standardize the entry of information and the pattern of operations in order to develop an integrated mechanized system which will exploit the resources in a group of libraries to serve users. It is recognized that mechanization would become more economical in library service if there were standardized entries, and that this would help to develop the network concept of library service and to extend library cooperation more readily on a reciprocal basis.

In 1964, the American Standards Association[19] developed draft standards on computer handling of information and circulated them widely for comments. Periodic review and revision of such standards may help to standardize techniques and operations within a reasonable limit.

The technological development of mechanical and electronic devices and of machine capabilities encouraged both federal and private agencies to develop centralized information services. The congressional hearings and reports by several presidential committees during the last eight years confirm this trend in information handling. A recent study of technical information centers reveals that a large number of government, academic, and private organizations are operating such centers and more than one hundred distinct subject areas are being covered. These information centers cover wide areas of current literature to produce computer-based announcement bulletins, indexes, abstracts, and other searching tools which an individual researcher can use.

The introduction of powerful electronic computers with the ability to handle information retrieval problems offers the possibility of storing huge collections of recorded information from which pertinent segments, correlated to the user's specific need, could be retrieved through the typing of a request on a console. The storage and retrieval of such an increased volume of literature brings about the need for research on the design of coding and indexing schemes. Continuing research is going on in the areas of automatic coding, indexing, and abstracting of documents. An application of Luhn's auto-encoding techniques has been taken as the basis for a research project at Herner and Company to design a vocabulary matrix that shows a combination of associated words and formulates likely term coordinations as an aid for further indexing and searching.

Since July, 1964, the Science Information Exchange in Washington has been working on the development of a mathematical model for computing unit computer costs for all searches or services performed by mechanized storage and retrieval activities.[20]

Among many other interesting developments in computer-based information retrieval, the project SHARP (Ships Analysis and Retrieval Projects) developed by John J. Nicolaus, the Librarian at the Bureau of Ships, merits particular mention. This computer-based system includes a complete package of information storage and retrieval systems, automatic production of the library's accession bulletin, catalog cards, automated inventory control and renewal of periodicals, and an automated projection of a users' subject interests register similar to SDI profiles.

The information retrieval system developed by Harold Borko and H. P. Burnaugh at the Systems Development Corporation in Santa Monica, California, which is known as BOLD (Bibliographic On-line Library Display) contemplates integrating cathode-ray-tube display consoles with teletypewriters and providing a number of remote user stations operating simultaneously by time-sharing in a large computer. The BOLD system has been designed to allow browsing through a magnetic tape file by subject category and displaying the authors, titles, and abstracts of the available documents on a CRT (Cathode-ray-tube). Document requests on a given subject are made by combining index terms to select the relevant documents from a display of the references on the CRT console.

The development of mechanized information retrieval and automated library service is correctly reflected in two recent surveys. The National Science Foundation[21] survey of technical libraries and information centers for descriptions of technical information systems based on the use of mechanical or electronic means of index manipulation, was included in the fourth issue of the compendia on non-conventional scientific and technical information systems in current use published in 1966. It shows one hundred percent increase in number over that in the previous issue of 1962. This is a definite indication of the increasing acceptance of the newer techniques in technical information systems.

In mid 1966, the Documentation Division of the Special Libraries Association and the Library Technology Program of the American Library Association, conducted a survey of the use of data processing equipment by libraries and information centers in the United States. The survey revealed that 638 libraries have mechanized one or more functions and 942 have approved plans for automation.

Eugene B. Jackson, in an article in *Special Libraries,* analyzed some of the significant data collected in this survey. The survey recorded that of the 638 libraries currently using data processing equipment, 75 percent are academic and special libraries. Further, 90 percent of the 942 libraries with authorized plans for automation fall under the same categories. Jackson observed that easy accessibility to data processing equipment influences the extent to which it is utilized. The increase of funds for acquisition of library materials as compared to funds available for processing the additions is causing concern and government libraries are influential in mechanization efforts out of proportion to their numbers because of the pioneering nature of their efforts.

In concluding the analysis Jackson remarked:

> The SLA-ALA/LTP survey forms a pioneer base-line inventory that can be of service to and be augmented by all concerned with every aspect of library mechanization. It does show where, which functions, authorized future installations, and the preference for mechanizing adminis-

trative functions over cataloging and public service functions.[22]

Lois C. McCune and Stephan R. Salmon recently compiled a bibliography of the literature on library automation and wrote in the introduction, "Emphasis has been placed primarily on recent writings; most of the literature that appeared before the early 1960's is now of historical interest."[23] This correctly expresses the awareness of librarians and information specialists of the need to change the pattern of investigation on computerized information retrieval, mechanized indexing, selective dissemination of information, and mechanization of routine library functions.

With a view to aiding the libraries actively engaged in or planning computerized library service, the American Library Association established the Information Science and Automation Division in January, 1966. The Division concerns itself

> ...with the development and application of electronic data processing techniques and the use of automated systems in all areas of library work and within this field will foster research, promote the development of appropriate standards, disseminate information, and provide a forum for the discussion of common problems.[24]

The Division is also exploring the possibilities of developing a Software and Computer Program Exchange (SCOPE) under which the library computer programs and related materials would be collected, updated periodically, and documented.

Bibliographical References

1 Shera, Jesse H. "Librarians against Machine" (Science 156(3776): 746-750, May 12, 1967).

2 Taylor, H. Selective Device (U.S. Patent No. 1, 165, 465, December 28, 1915).

3 Soper, H. E. Means for Compiling Tabular and Statistical Data (U. S. Patent No. 1, 351, 692, August 31, 1920).

4 Goldberg, E. Statistical Machines (U. S. Patent No. 1, 838, 389, December 29, 1931).

5 Parker, R. H. "The Punch Card Method in Circulation Work" (Library Journal 61:903-905 December, 1936).

6 Quigley, Margery "Automatic Book Charging" (Library Journal 66:803 September 15, 1941).

7 Pratt, E. Carl "International Business Machines Use in Circulation Department, Univ. of Florida Library" (Library Journal 67: 302-303, April, 1942).

8 Dewey, Harry T. "Punched Card Catalogues: Theory and techniques" (American Documentation 10:36-50, January, 1959).

9 Draeger, R. H. A Proposed Photoelectric Selecting Mechanism for the Sorting of Bibliographic Abstract Entries from 35 mm Film (Documentation Institute of Science Service, Document no. 62, July, 1935).

10 Bush, Vannevar "As We May Think" (Atlantic Monthly 176:101-108, July, 1945).

11 Shaw, Ralph R. The Use of Photography for Clerical Routines. A report to the American Council of Learned Societies, Washington, D. C., 1953.

12 Hand, W. J., Moore, F. M. and Runge, Gretchen "The Special Library of the Future (Special Libraries 42(1):13, January, 1951).

13 Shaw, Ralph R. "Machine and the Bibliographical Problems of the Twentieth Century." Windsor Lecture at the University of Illinois, March, 1950.

14 Moors, Calvin N. "The next Twenty Years in Information Retrieval: Some goals and predictions" (American Documentation 11:229-236, 1960).

15 Science, Government and Information The Responsibilities of the Technical Community and the Government in the Transfer of Information, January 10, 1963, p. 84.

16 Lipetz, Ben-Ami "Information Storage and Retrieval" (Sci. Am., 215(3):224-242, September, 1966).

17 American Library Association The Use of Data Processing Equipment in Circulation Control (Library Technology Reports--Circulation systems, July, 1965, p. 24).

18 Statements provided for the National Science Foundation Report, Current Research and Development in Scientific Documentation No. 14, p. 297-298 (National Science Foundation Report No. NSF-66-17).

19 Communications of the ACM, vol. 7, no. 5 (May, 1964), p. 284-287 and no. 6 (June, 1964), p. 333-339.

20 National Science Foundation Current Research and Development in Scientific Documentation, no. 14, p. 438.

21 National Science Foundation Nonconventional Scientific and Technical Information Systems in Current Use, no. 4, December, 1966.

22 Jackson, Eugene B. "The Use of Data Processing Equipment by Libraries and Information Centers." The significant results of the SLA-LTP Survey (Special Libraries, May-June, 1967, p. 317-327).

23 McCune, Lis C. and Salmon, Stephen R. "Bibliography of Library Automation" (ALA Bulletin, June, 1967, p. 674-694).

24 Salmon, Stephen R. "Information Science and Automation: the Newest Division" (ALA Bulletin 61(6):637-641, June, 1967).

14. Library Education and Information Science

The Education for special librarianship has remained a subject for discussion and debate since the inception of the Special Libraries Association in 1909. One group voiced their criticism by pointing out that the principles and techniques of general librarianship as expressed in the core curriculum are not readily applicable to special library practice and the library schools have not accorded special librarianship the attention it deserves. Another equally strong group, however, argued that the special librarianship constitutes only several specialized applications of the principles and techniques common to all areas of librarianship. They went on to say that the necessity for special instruction has been occasioned by the particular contexts in which special library services are to be provided. True specialization, they said, can be attained only through internship within library specialities. Such dialogue continued but no dynamic education program could be formalized for several decades.

Librarians, however, gradually began to play an increased role in the process of systematization and communication when the first conference on scientific information, sponsored by the Royal Society in 1948, emphasized the need for integrating scientific and technical information and bibliographic work with the different stages of increased scientific research and experimental work. The recommendations of the conference encouraged several active groups to give systematic thought to deeper analysis in indexing and to experiment with machine methods for the rapid retrieval of a larger volume of scientific and technical information.

The growing volume of scientific literature in a variety of formats, the increased acceptance of the newer communication channel in the form of technical reports, research memoranda, the deeper insight into the several indexing methods, and the technological developments for automated information storage and retrieval since the 1950's further amplified the fact that special librarians needed a coordinated, intensive, formalized, continuing program of re-education in newer concepts of special library and documentation services.

Systematic thought on the training of documentalists, however, came only after 1950. Jesse H. Shera and Margaret E. Egan, in the first issue of American Documentation in 1950, stated:

> There is in this country no provision for specific training of documentalists. Those who are now active in the various fields related to documentation have received their training in one of three ways: (1) training for librarianship; (2) training for archivists; (3) advanced training in a subject field.
>
> Many of the activities coming under the term "documentation" are carried on by the staff of the indexing and abstracting services and by special librarians. For both groups, training in the specific field is considered essential but usually insufficient.
>
> In spite of the excellent training offered by many universities in the substantive matter of the subject fields, the bibliographic aspects are too frequently neglected and there has been considerable pressure on the library schools to include special training for documentalists in their program.[1]

The Library School of Western Reserve University was the first to offer a formal course in documentation, which started in the academic year 1949-50. The success of this training program encouraged Western Reserve to establish, in 1955, the first Center for Documentation and Communication Research, as the research wing of the School of Library Science, and to adopt a four-pronged program--education, research, liaison, and operational service. Dean Shera expressed the hope that the experience gained from the continuing research at the Center would "... enrich the curriculum and provide the profession with more adequately trained librarians."[2]

At the initial stage the Center organized two formal courses of training--machine literature searching, and language engineering. The increasing acceptance of the information center concept since the late 1950's and the proliferation of such specialized centers in government agencies, research bodies, and industrial companies for information processing and dissemination of scientific information, created a new cadre under a variety of names--Information Scientist,

Information Specialist, Literature Scientist, or Literature Analyst. Though the American Documentation Institute came into existence in the United States as early as 1937 for the promotion and systematization of documentation activities, the words "documentation" and "documentalist" were generally avoided because of the variety of ways in which they were used and because of the numerous interpretations of their meaning. As information processing is viewed to encompass a broader spectrum of activities than defined by the special library, scientific workers who preferred desk work to laboratory work had a better chance of being employed in the handling of scientific information.

In 1962, the Education Committee of the Special Library Association reported that in the domain of special libraries and documentation service an increasing proportion of the work of handling and processing information is being done by persons who do not have formal library education and training. This is more evident in the field of documentation, especially in industry, government agencies and research organizations.

The Committee recommended that the training for special librarianship should include a knowledge of the new concepts of information storage and retrieval, which should include not only an understanding of the various types of mechanical equipment, but also the basic principles of various systems.[3]

A. J. Goldwyn,[4] at a conference in Warrenton, Virginia, very correctly said that the main objective of a course in library automation given in the library schools should be to indoctrinate with an attitude rather than a specific skill in system analysis which rapidly gets outmoded.

It is only in recent years that library schools have begun to emphasize new developments in information transfer technology in their formal courses and regard documentation and information retrieval as integral parts of the total field of librarianship.

The question of the formalization of a sound academic curriculum for information handling personnel within and outside of library schools has also become vital.

Don R. Swanson at a recent conference on library education

very correctly said,

> Library education must be built upon sound intellectual foundations, but at the same time it cannot ignore the vocational skills needed in the practice of librarianship. The vocational needs of the profession are great, and the skills are not difficult to recognize; but their intellectual content is often obscure and subject to divided opinion. [5]

On the issue of training programs for information scientists or information specialists, the Symposium on Technical Information Personnel, held in New York in April, 1960, and participated in by scientists, science information specialists and librarians, detailed twelve principal areas for science information work. They failed to identify the functions of a special librarian or an information scientist and concluded that the duties of both very often overlap.

Cohan and Craven[6] in their studies of the "personnel question" in the domain of scientific information, felt that to solve the problems of training efficient information specialists there should be a one-year graduate curriculum leading to an M.S. degree in Information Science. They further detailed that the course of 15 credit hours spread over three semesters.

Upon the initiative of the Georgia Institute of Technology, the National Science Foundation sponsored Conferences on Training Science Information Specialists in October, 1961 and in April, 1962, discussed varied approaches to training persons engaged in science information work and categorized three distinct groups of personnel needed in this field: (1) science librarians; (2) technical literature analysts; and (3) information scientists. The conference also emphasized that the needed personnel should take a variety of courses--short courses, in-service training programs and formal training leading to the Master's or Doctor's degree.

The conference recommended that for science librarians the present Master's degree curriculum should be oriented more strongly towards scientific and technical literature. The education program for technical literature analysts should place emphasis on information science as a major and some additional work in a technical specialty. Alternatively, the technical subject may be emphasized and information work may be taken as a minor. The education requirement for

Library Education 151

information scientists includes training in mathematics, mathematical linguistics, computers, and information science proper which could be handled best at the doctoral level.

Following the conference at the Georgia Institute of Technology in 1962, a number of conferences were held during the past five years by the Special Libraries Association, the American Documentation Institute, and other bodies at the national and international levels to determine the intellectual foundation of education both in library science and information sciences. Discussion at several conferences has made it quite apparent that polarization of training in library science and information science is not desirable since both have the same root and same ends. The fields of information science, information technology, information retrieval, and documentation are rather an integral part of library science.

Joseph C. Donohue,[7] in 1965, analyzed library school courses to find each school's involvement in information science education. His study shows that 77 percent of the 34 schools who responded to his inquiry offer at least one course in information science. Twelve schools offer only one course, 8 schools offer 3 courses, and in 8 schools 75 percent of all courses relate to information science. All these courses vary in nature and coverage.

Alan M. Rees in a recent paper, "Information Science in Library School Curricula," revealed that 17 schools now offer a total of 25 courses in the area of data processing and library automation under a variety of course titles. The courses mostly cover system analysis, flow charting, and theory and application of automation to library routine processes. In the areas of documentation and information storage, retrieval, and dissemination, 19 schools offer a total of 39 courses under different titles which cover: design of retrieval systems, acquisition, subject analysis including indexing and abstracting, structure of indexing languages, coding, file organization, question analysis and search strategy, dissemination, testing and evaluation of retrieval systems, and administration of information centers. Besides these courses, six schools offer 13 courses on information science research methodology, which cover the study of principles of mathematics, logic, linguistics, statistics, and other sciences and their application to research in library and communication related problems.

Rees concluded that

> Most teaching efforts are concentrated in the area of data processing in the library (library automation); a lesser amount in documentation and information retrieval; and very little research that is in information science in the strict sense.[8]

The University of Chicago, the University of Pittsburgh, Western Reserve University, and Florida State University have formalized subcurricula on information science within the degree program of the library schools. The courses provide for specialization at both the master's and the doctoral level.

The continuing research program in different areas of documentation at the Center for Documentation and Communication Research, Western Reserve University, is increasingly reflected in the Center's academic curriculum. Ten formal courses in documentation, which are closely allied with the core program for the M. S. degree in Library Science, are now provided by the Center. These courses are titled as follows: Documentation, Information Retrieval Systems, Parts I and II, Information Processing on Computers, Introduction to Information Retrieval Theory, Automated Language Processing, Theory of Classification, Specialized Information Centers and Services, Automation of Library Processes and Procedures, and Special Studies in Documentation. The Ph. D. program, which is interdisciplinary, is a combination of library science and other subject fields, thus giving the student a comprehensive knowledge of the information sciences.[9]

The University of California at Los Angeles, the Drexel Institute of Technology, the Center for Information Sciences at Lehigh University, University of Michigan, and the Georgia Institute of Technology have developed a degree course in information science at the Master's level.

In order to place systems analysis, data processing, and information science in proper perspective with the traditions and professional requirements of librarianship, the University of California at Los Angeles introduced four courses: (1) Introduction to Library Systems Analysis, to introduce students to the principles of systems analysis and data processing with emphasis on those issues which concern librarians; (2) Data Processing in the Library, which provides further study of data processing applications to library operations, with emphasis on computer programming and methods analysis; (3) Methods of Information System Analysis and Design, to provide detailed study of the methods and techniques of systems analysis as applied to information systems; and (4) Seminar on Information Science, to encourage advanced students to investigate and experiment with different information transfer problems. The core courses--System Integration; Usage of Information; Organization and Operation of Information Systems; and Equipment and Design of Information Services--are covered by the School of Library Science. The remaining interdisciplinary courses are offered by the Departments of Mathematics, Philosophy, Language, Business Administration, Engineering and others.

The Drexel Information Science curriculum is separate from the library science curriculum though both are in the School of Library Science. The course is designed to train science information practitioners, and five major areas of specialization are offered: publication, science bibliography, management, science or technology, and instrumentation.

Since the Fall of 1964, the Center for Information Sciences at Lehigh University has been offering an interdisciplinary master's program to train information scientists. The courses include the areas of analysis of information, information systems design, general linguistics, syntactic concepts, logico-mathematical theories of retrieval, and the environment of information systems.

Courses in the University's Departments of Engineering, Mathematics, Social Relations, Economics, Psychology and others are part of the curriculum.

The University of Michigan has designed a curriculum in communication sciences for training of information scientists at the master's level. The program includes the use of computers for investigating languages and symbolic processes, and also the development and use of languages to study the nature of computers; instrumentation for speech analysis, and information processing by conventional and non-conventional methods.

The Georgia Institute of Technology offers a degree course on information science, for the technical literature analyst, outside the Library School. This curriculum is designed for the development of competence in three broad areas: (1) science information, (2) modern languages and (3) advanced subject specialization in a particular field of science or engineering. The courses on science information aim to investigate the properties and behavior of information, the forces governing the flow of information, and the means of processing information for optimum accessibility and usability. The process includes the origination, dissemination, collection, organization, storage, retrieval, interpretation, and use of information.

Universities continue to develop curricula in documentation and information science. Though there is no general agreement on the courses to be offered Robert M. Hayes, in a recent paper "Data Processing in the Library School Curriculum," made a comparison of the training on data processing and information systems now offered at 35 universities, including the programs in 9 non-library schools. The comparison is based upon four broad courses of the curriculum for the M. S. degree in Information Science at UCLA. These four courses are: (1) Methods Analysis for Libraries and Library Systems Analysis; (2) Mechanized Information Retrieval and Data Processing in the Library; (3) Information Systems Analysis: systems problems in application to different information problems; and (4) Research. (Hayes excluded the courses for special librarianship, information specialization, and documentation.) The table below analyzes the data recorded in Hayes' paper.

Courses	No. of Universities	Percentage of the Total 35
1	7	20%
2	24	68.5%
3	21	60%
4	15	42.8%
1 + 2	6	17.1%
2 + 3	12	34.3%
3 + 4	14	40%

Courses	No. of Universities	Percentage of the Total 35
2 + 3 + 4	9	25. 7%
1 + 2 + 3 + 4	5	14. 3%

The table shows that though Course 1 is provided in 7 universities (20% of the total), Courses 2 and 3 are provided in more than 60% of the universities. This means that universities are giving more attention to mechanized information retrieval, information system analysis, and automated library operations. Research courses have been provided in 42. 8 percent of the universities. All four courses are offered in only five universities (14. 3 percent of the total).

In addition to the formal courses offered at the institutions of higher learning within and outside of the library schools, educational and professional groups are organizing short-term training programs, workshops and seminars on computer systems and other related problems of specialized information handling. Such workshop and seminar programs have largely increased in recent years due to pressure for this type of training.

Bibliographical References

1   Shera, Jesse H. and Egan, Margaret E. "Documentation in the United States" (American Documentation 1(1):8-12, January, 1950).

2   Shera, Jesse H. "Librarianship in a High Key" (ALA Bulletin, vol. 50, February, 1956).

3   Special Libraries Association "Committee Reports 1961/62." (Special Libraries 53(7):407-408, September, 1962).

4   Goldwyn, A. J. "The Advance of Automation: Its implications for Library Education" (Library Journal, July, 1963, p. 2640-2643).

5   Swanson, Don R. "The Intellectual Foundation of Library Education" (Library Quarterly 34(4):289-294, October, 1964).

6   Cohan, Leonard and Craven, Kenneth Science Information Personnel (New York Science Information, 1961).

7   Donohue, Joseph C. "Librarianship and the Science of Information" (American Documentation 17(3):120-123, July, 1966).

8 Rees, Alan M. and Riccio, Dorothy "Information Science in Library School Curricula," 1967 (Mimeographed).

9 Rees, Alan M. and Sarachvic, Fefko "Teaching Documentation at Western Reserve University."

10 Hayes, Robert M. "Data Processing in the Library School Curriculum" (ALA Bulletin, June, 1967, p. 662-669).

15. Trends in Research and Development

As stated in an earlier chapter, after the Royal Society Conference on Scientific Information in 1948, several active groups of librarians and scientists began to give systematic thought to deeper analysis in indexing methods and to experimentation with data processing equipment for bibliographic control of the increased volume of literature in a variety of formats. This was long before the education on newer information retrieval systems could be formalized. In earlier years, in the absence of adequate financial support and facilities, research and experimentation on information retrieval remained mostly at the individual level and outside the universities. This situation, however, quickly changed after the establishment of the National Science Foundation (NSF) in 1950.

From the beginning, the National Science Foundation recognized the need for improvement of science information systems. Early in its history it began to support research on the process of information and document handling, on improved methods of abstracting and indexing, on use of mechanical and electronic data processing equipment for information retrieval, on methods for speeding up the publication of the results of research and for fostering the translation of foreign scientific documents.

To coordinate research and developmental activities in information science and to disseminate the research results, the NSF in November, 1958, published the first of a series of pamphlets on the scientific information activities of federal agencies. And, in order to communicate national and international developments in scientific and technical information retrieval, the Foundation began issuing a bimonthly publication, Science Information News, in February, 1959. This later became Scientific Information Notes. Current Research and Development in Scientific Documentation and Non-conventional Scientific and Technical Information Systems in Current Use are two NSF publications which record statements of research activities in scientific documentation and related subjects, and describe technical information systems based on mechanical or electronic data processing equipment.

The President's Science Advisory Committee directed the Foundation to take the lead in bringing about effective coordination of the various scientific information activities within the federal government. NSF, however, could not successfully coordinate the major science information activities or provide coherence in the growing and often uncorrelated matrix of federal information sources and dissemination system. In 1962, the Federal Council and its Committee on Scientific and Technical Information, took over this responsibility, under the auspices of the Office of Science and Technology.

Several congressional hearings and presidential committees on science information[1-7] in recent years have recognized that the communication of technical information is an integral part of research and development and stressed the need for a coordinated program of research and development in information science and information technology. President Kennedy, in the foreword of the Weinberg Report, wrote:

> One of the major opportunities for enhancing the effectiveness of our national scientific and technical effort and the efficiency of the Government management of research and development lies in the improvement of our ability to communicate information about current research efforts and the results of past efforts.[3]

This increased awareness and financial support from federal and private bodies to creat a dynamic and flexible information strategy encouraged scientists, linguists, system analysts, and library experts in academic institutions and in information centers, to undertake research projects and experimentation on theoretical and applied problems on information transfer and document handling and to develop mechanisms for more efficient information systems.

To exploit the developing computer technology for this newer dimension of information retrieval and dissemination, research is going on in both the machine area and the intellectual area. In the machine area, experiments are being made on character-recognition and optical input; miniaturization and the use of computer technology for high density storage and retrieval; increased use of random access computers; special software packages for information processing; increasing the use of teleprocessing techniques; and remote facsimile or other means for reproducing source documents. In the intellectual area, research is going on in the mechanization of classification and indexing; automatic abstracting and interpretation of texts; new teaching programs and development of standardized methods for communicating thought and meaning; and the correlation of human thought processes with mechanical devices and artificial intelligence systems.

During my short stay in the United States, I had an opportunity to examine a few selected research projects, which include INTREX and TIP at the Massachusetts Institute of Technology; MARC at the Library of Congress; machine methods and relevance studies at the Comparative Systems Laboratory, Center for Documentation and Communication Research, Western Reserve University and a few others. To get some idea of present trends in research activities on information and document handling, I scanned the statements of research projects in Current Research and Development in Scientific Documentation (CRDSD).[8] The CRDSD reports are not complete and there are undoubtedly numerous projects which are not included in CRDSD. However, a statistical analysis of the recorded statements under each area of research is definite enough to give a broad idea of the trends of developmental activities and research interests.

The research statements in the earlier issues (Nos. 8 to 13) of CRDSD are grouped into nine broad categories which center around major investigations in information handling problems and related subjects. They are as follows: (1) Information needs and uses; (2) Information storage and retrieval; (3) Machine translation; (4) Equipment; (5) Character and pattern recognition; (6) Speech analysis and synthesis; (7) Linguistic and lexicographic research; (8) Artificial intelligence; and (9) Psychological studies.

The subjects and topics covered under each category are:

1. Information needs and uses: Studies and analysis of information needs of scientists and the uses made of scientific literature, the mode and manner in which scientists communicate, observation and analysis of cited references, and the behavioral and sociological aspects of

scientific communication are the major topics.

2. Information storage and retrieval: The design and operation of new operation systems; development of mechanized methods for processing and retrieval in natural language; comparative testing of operating retrieval systems, investigation of problems involved in analyzing, processing, storing and searching; and theoretical studies on information search systems, including various indexing methods and classification schemes.

3. Mechanical translation: Research and experimentation on the application of computers for automatic translation from one natural language to another, and linguistic studies on the characteristics of the languages are the topics in this area.

4. Equipment: Development and experimental design of newer machines suitable for information handling, including communication media are grouped in this area.

5. Related researches: The five sub-areas grouped as related researches are not problems directly involved in documentation activities. The solution of some of the problems, however, is likely to have an impact on future documentation.

5. 1. Character and pattern recognition: Experiments on the computer-based operations to optical pattern recognition, coding, retrieval translation of signs to corresponding data or to other sign systems are the major topics. The applications include: (1) character (letters and conventional signs) recognition; (2) coding of geometric configurations in patterns; (3) pictorial image recognition and interpretation; (4) graph recognition.

5. 2. Speech analysis and synthesis: The area of research in recognition of speech patterns is concerned with physiologic, acoustical, and phonetical aspects of sound generated; experimental design of the mechanism for identification of the speaker through analysis of speech and synthesizing the verbal words to a computer simulation.

5. 3. Linguistics and lexicographic research: Studies on linguistic structure, syntactic, morphological, and semantic analysis to develop techniques for recognizing and manipulating the structures of natural language to aid research on automatic abstracting, indexing, content analysis, etc., and mechanical translation are covered in this

area of research.

5. 4. Artificial intelligence: Research in this area is concentrated on simulating the complex information processing activities involved in human cognition and the neurophysiological mechanisms that underlie them; experiments in this area also involve the interpretation and interrelationship in neural networks as they process incoming stimuli. Mathematical, physical, neurophysiological, and psychological models of these processes and mechanism, and computer and computer simulation techniques are being used as primary tools for testing the models to gain new insight into the nature of these processes and mechanism.

5. 5. Psychological studies: The major topics in this area deal with the nature and development of information processing in human perception, memory, learning, and problem solving.

In the current issue (No. 14) of the CRDSD (published in 1966), the research statements are grouped under the following nine redefined categories which consider the present mode of research and development: (1) Information needs and uses; (2) Document creation and copying; (3) Language analysis; (4) Translation; (5) Abstracting, classification, coding and indexing; (6) System design; (7) Analysis and evaluation; (8) Pattern recognition; and (9) Adaptive systems.

The areas of research activities as delineated in the CRDSD categories are not mutually exclusive or exhaustive; they represent a pragmatic description of those areas, and these boundaries often merge or overlap.

The research projects recorded in CRDSD (Nos. 8 and No. 13) covering 1960 and 1963, have been tabulated and analyzed. (See Tables I and II.)

Table I presents the number of research statements reported in CRDSD by areas of research with figures for U. S. projects and foreign projects. Approximately 70 percent of the recorded researches are of U. S. origin and this pattern is more or less consistent all through. The total number of projects increased from 195 to 495, which means an increase of 154 percent over a period of four years. The U. S. projects increased from 137 to 337, an increase of 146 percent. The foreign projects increased from 58 to 158, an increase

Table I: Number of Statements on Research and Developments in Scientific Documentation in CRDSD

		CRDSD [8] (May 1961)			CRDSD [13] (November 1964)		
	Categories	U.S.	foreign	total	U.S.	foreign	total
1	Information needs and uses	21	1	22	46	12	58
2	Information storage and retrieval	33	18	51	118	41	159
3	Machine translation	13	19	32	17	34	51
4	Equipment	14	0	14	20	4	24
5	Related research	56	20	76	136	67	203
.1	Character & pattern recognition	20	7	27	39	15	54
.2	Speech analysis & synthesis	8	3	11	22	9	31
.3	Linguistic & lexicographic research	9	7	16	27	31	58
.4	Artificial intelligence	17	3	20	37	11	48
.5	Psychological studies	2	0	2	11	1	12
	Total	137	58	195	337	158	495
	Percentage of U.S. statements	70.3			68.1		

Source: National Science Foundation - Current Research and Development in Scientific Documentation, Nos. 8 and 13.

Table II: Percentage of CRDSD Statements, by areas of research

		CRDSD [8]			CRDSD [13]		
	Categories	U.S.	foreign	total	U.S.	foreign	total
1	Information needs and uses	15.3	1.7	11.3	13.7	7.6	11.7
2	Information storage and retrieval	24.1	31.0	26.1	35.0	26.0	32.1
3	Machine translation	9.5	32.8	16.4	5.0	21.5	10.3
4	Equipment	10.2	-	7.2	5.9	2.5	4.9
5	Related research	40.9	34.5	39.0	40.4	42.4	41.0
.1	Character and pattern recognition	14.6	12.1	13.9	11.6	9.5	10.9
.2	Speech analysis and synthesis	5.8	5.2	5.6	6.5	5.7	6.3
.3	Linguistic & lexicographic research	6.6	12.1	8.2	8.0	19.6	11.7
.4	Artificial intelligence	12.4	5.2	10.3	11.0	7.0	9.7
.5	Psychological studies	1.5	-	1.0	3.3	0.6	2.4

Source: National Science Foundation - Current Research and Development in Scientific Documentation, Nos. 8 and 13.

Table III: Number and Percentage Share of the U. S. Research Statements and Their Change Factor from CRDSD [8] to CRDSD [13]

		CRDSD [8]		CRDSD [13]		change in [13] over [8]	
	Categories	no.	p. c.	no.	p. c.	no.	percentage of increase
1	Information needs and uses	21	15.3	46	13.7	25	119.0
2	Information storage and retrieval	33	24.1	118	35.0	85	257.0
3	Machine translation	13	9.5	17	5.0	4	31.0
4	Equipment	14	10.2	20	5.9	6	43.0
5	Related research	56	40.9	136	40.4	80	143.0
.1	Character and pattern recognition	20	14.6	39	11.6	19	95.0
.2	Speech analysis and synthesis	8	5.8	22	6.5	14	175.0
.3	Linguistic & lexicographic research	9	6.6	27	8.0	18	200.0
.4	Artificial intelligence	17	12.4	37	11.0	20	118.0
.5	Psychological studies	2	1.5	11	3.3	9	450.0
	Total	137	100.0	337	100.0	200	146.0

Source: National Science Foundation - Current Research and Development in Scientific Documentation, Nos. 8 and 13.

of 171 percent. This higher rate of increase of foreign projects may be due to better reporting than an actual higher increase, or to the fact that a smaller number of projects more easily increases by a higher percentage.

Table II gives the percentage share of the CRDSD statements by areas of research to identify the relative increase or decrease of research activities in different areas. It may be seen that the information storage and retrieval always remained the major area of research activities (sharing the highest percentage) both in the U.S. and foreign countries. The percentage share of the five areas of related research remained more or less constant, sharing around 40 percent of the total projects.

Table III presents the number and percentage share of research projects undertaken in the United States. The research interest in the area of information storage and retrieval is much higher than in other areas as evident from the systematic increase by 257 percent within the reference period of four years.

Table IV presents an analysis of the types of organizations engaged in research activities. The 499 statements in CRDSD No. 13 show that 35.9 percent of the research and experiments are carried out by "Industry," 34.5 percent by "University," 13.6 percent by "Research Institutes and Societies," and 8.0 percent each by "Government Research Groups," and by "Information Groups and Others." "University" and "Industry" together account for over 70 percent of the total research projects.

In the area of information needs and uses "Industry" and "University" both register 25.9 percent. In information storage and retrieval, "Industry" has given more attention than "University." "Industry" is carrying out 38.4 percent of the researches while "University" only 26.4 percent.

The majority of research projects on machine translations are conducted in "universities," sharing 56.9 percent of the total projects. In the equipment area 75.0 percent of the research projects are carried on in "Industry," while only 12.5 percent are being carried on by "Government Research Groups." 41.1 percent of the related research is done in universities and 37.7 percent in "Industry" but it is interesting to note that 63.0 percent of the research on "Character and Pattern Recognition" is done in "Industry" and only a minor part (14.8 percent) in "Universities." In the area of "Speech Analysis and Synthesis," "Industry" and "Universities" are equally responsive, each carrying 45.1 percent of the total projects. 48.3 percent of the "Linguistic and Lexicographic Research" is undertaken in "Universities" and 31.0 percent in "Research Institutes and Societies," "Industry" sharing only 13.8 percent. In the area of "Artificial Intelligence," "Universities" are conducting 47.1 percent of the researches, and "Industry" 41.1 percent. Research interest in the area of "Psychological Studies" is still very limited and out of 13 projects "Universities" are conducting 11 ("Industry" and "Research Institutes" are doing one each).

It may be concluded from this quantitative analysis that there are signs of a levelling off in the rate of increase in information research activities in several areas. Research interest in the area of

Table IV: Number and Percentage Share of the Research Statements by Types of Organizations

Types of organization	1 no	1 p.c.	2 no	2 p.c.	3 no	3 p.c.	4 no	4 p.c.	5 no	5 p.c.	5.1 no	5.1 p.c.	5.2 no	5.2 p.c.	5.3 no	5.3 p.c.	5.4 no	5.4 p.c.	5.5 no	5.5 p.c.	Total (1 to 5) no	Total p.c.
(1)	(2)	(3)	(4)	(5)	(6)	(7)	(8)	(9)	(10)	(11)	(12)	(13)	(14)	(15)	(16)	(17)	(18)	(19)	(20)	(21)	(22)	(23)
1 Industry	15	25.9	61	38.4	7	13.7	18	75.0	78	37.7	34	63.0	14	45.1	8	13.8	21	41.1	1	7.7	179	35.9
2 University	15	25.9	42	26.4	29	56.9	1	4.2	85	41.1	8	14.8	14	45.1	28	48.3	24	47.1	11	84.6	172	34.5
3 Research institutes and societies	11	19.0	18	11.3	8	15.7	2	8.3	29	14.0	5	9.3	2	6.5	18	31.0	3	5.9	1	7.7	68	13.6
4 Government research groups	7	12.1	17	10.7	5	9.8	3	12.5	8	3.8	5	9.3	1	3.3	-	-	2	3.9	-	-	40	8.0
5 Information groups and others	10	17.2	21	13.2	2	3.9	-	-	7	3.4	2	3.7	-	-	4	6.9	1	2.0	-	-	40	8.0
Total	58		159		51		24		207		54		31		58		51		13		499	100.0

Source: CRDSD No. 13 wherein 495 statements have been recorded. The difference in total is accounted for joint contracts on some projects.

"Information Storage and Retrieval," however, still continues to be strong. "Universities" and "Industries" take an equal interest in research and the development of information science and technology, with more than two thirds of the research projects conducted in these two types of organizations.

The team of experts appointed by the Committee on Scientific and Technical Information (COSATI) in their recent study of national systems for scientific and technical information, stressed the need for a coordinated and balanced program of research and development in different areas of information science and technology. The COSATI Report[9] identified the following areas where increased research is needed.

1. <u>User studies</u>: Research is needed to determine both the recognized and the unrecognized needs of users and to devise means of making the information systems more responsive.

2. <u>Document representation</u>: Studies are needed on how documents can be condensed and represented by both manual and automated means, to serve more effectively in providing current awareness materials and in aiding retrospective searches.

3. <u>Evaluation tools and techniques</u>: Tools and techniques are needed for assessing the adequacy of information systems and their continuing ability to serve their users.

4. <u>Communication of information</u>: Research is needed to determine the most appropriate means for the system to facilitate information transfer through informal or oral means as well as through formal documents. Research is needed to clarify the role of documentation and other media of information transfer in the growth of science and technology.

5. <u>Equipment for information handling</u>: There is a requirement for research and development directed toward the provision of automated equipment aids for the storage, manipulation, and transmission of information to users.

Bibliographical References

1 Baker, W.O. (ed.) Improving the availability of scientific and technical information in the United States. Panel Report of the

Trends in Research   167

President's Science Advisory Committee, December, 1958.

2 Crawford, J. H. and others Scientific and technical communications in the Government. (Task Force Report to the President's Special Assistant for Science and Technology. AD -299-545, April, 1962.

3 Weinberg, A. M. Science, Government and Information: The responsibilities of the Technical Community and the Government in the Transfer of Information. Report of the President's Science Advisory Committee, January, 1963.

4 Licklider, J. C. R. Report by the Office of Science and Technology (OTS) Panel on Scientific and Technical Communications to Dr. Donald F. Horning, President's Science Advisor, February, 1965.

5 U. S. Congress, House of Representatives, Committee on Government operations, Select Committee on Government Research: Documentation and dissemination of research and development results. 88th Congress 2nd Session, November, 1964. (The Elliot Report)

6 U. S. Congress, House of Representatives, Committee on Government operations: Automatic Data Processing Equipment. 89th Congress 1st Session. March, 1965. (The Brooks Report)

7 U. S. Congress, Senate, Committee on Government operations: Summary of activities toward interagency co-ordination. 89th Congress, 1st Session. June, 1965. (The Humphrey Report)

8 National Science Foundation Current Research and Development in Scientific Documentation, Nos. 8-11, 13.

9 Federal Council for Science and Technology - Committee on Scientific and Technical Information: Recommendations for National Document Handling Systems in Science and Technology. AD-624-560, November, 1965.

Appendix

1   Libraries and Technical Information Centers in Industry
 .1   Bell Laboratories, Technical Information Libraries
 .2   ESSO, Technical Information Division
 .3   SK&F, Science Information Division
 .4   LMSC, Technical Information Center
 .5   IBM, ASDD, Research Library
 .6   IBM, TJWRC, Research Library
 .7   IBM, Technical Information Retrieval Center

2   Technical Information Centers under Federal Agencies
 .1   NASA, Scientific and Technical Information Systems
 .2   NLM, MEDLARS Information Systems Division

3   Technical Information Centers under Private Agency
 .1   Institute for Scientific Information

4   Special Libraries
 .1   Library, School of Medicine, Washington University
 .2   John Crerar Library

5   Developmental Projects
 .1   Library of Congress, Automation Program
 .2   Library of Congress, National Referral Center
 .3   MIT, Technical Information Project (TIP)
 .4   MIT Project: INTREX

Bell Telephone Laboratories
Technical Information Libraries

Bell Laboratories has the largest industrial research library in the United States. The library system embraces a network of 19 library units, in ten states, serving more than 5,000 scientists, engineers, and technicians engaged in the Company's research and development activities. Though each library is oriented to meet the special needs of that particular center, acquisition, cataloging, publication, translation, technical reports, and systems studies are centralized to provide the same standards of service and integrated library facilities.

The total book resources of six of the major library units have been integrated in a union card catalog system. A computer-generated printed catalog is being developed to extend this facility to all Bell Laboratory facilities. The library system is provided with computer-produced catalogs and indexes to journal holdings, company reports, computer programs, translations, and other information.

All the libraries and library users have access to CORNET, the corporate network linking Bell Laboratories locations together, as well as to the American Telephone and Telegraph Company and to Western Electric Company. The larger libraries are equipped with a Telereference facility which is a message recording system available to any employee at any time from anywhere.

A system that links the three largest libraries--at Murray Hill, Holmdel, and Whippany, New Jersey--to an on-line, real-time computer, services over 400,000 transactions a year in these three libraries. It handles library loans, reservation of materials and inquiries.

A group of system analysts and programmers are working in the Bell Laboratories Library to design and implement new information handling techniques and services with computer-aided systems. The intellectual part of the documentation activities is handled by senior scientists who are working on the Library staff as information scientists and literature analysts. This group handles more difficult information requests, prepares comprehensive and critical literature searches on demand, compiles bibliographies, and carries on continuing reviews of the literature on subject areas in which the Company is interested. Several foreign language experts are also attached to the Library to translate documents from other languages. The translators provided more than 7,000 pages of translations of technical documents in 1966. The photoduplicating service copied 170,000 articles and technical reports in 1966 to meet the researchers' needs.

To disseminate the current technical literature, eight announcement bulletins are regularly issued by the Technical Information Libraries. Three of them are computer-printed and indexed and several others are in the process of being transferred to a computer base. The <u>Library Bulletin</u> announces new books, journals, and other reading materials and also lists TIL translations and bibliographies. The scope of some of the other bulletins is wide and general in nature but some are on specific subjects. The bulletins cover computer programs, published literature on the physical sciences, biological sciences, management literature, and government documents both unclassified and classified. Bell Laboratories' internal scientific and technical communications are covered in <u>Technical Memoranda Index</u> and <u>Bell Laboratories Talks and Papers</u>. These bulletins announced over 83,000 items in 1966. Six other bibliographical publications are issued by the Technical Information Libraries at irregular intervals or prepared on specific requests. The Technical Reports Center at the Whippany Library is the clearing house for technical documents. The Center organizes, announces, and distributes the technical reports collected from government agencies, military organizations, and other sources.

Another computer-aided alerting service, the MERCURY system, has been developed for the dissemination of internal technical documents to the Bell Laboratories' scientists and engineers. This mechanism has systematized the distribution of papers among those who have expressed an interest in receiving papers on specified subjects, or projects, or by specified authors or departments. The MERCURY thesaurus is a hierarchically structured subject vocabulary especially designed for the purpose, and the matching of the document against the researcher's profile is done by computer. The computer generates the distribution list and printed labels for mailing the document and prints an explanation to tell the recipient why he is receiving that document.

In Bell Technical Information Libraries about 200 different library operations and services have been automated. These include permutation and citation indexing; the production of bibliographies, catalogs and announcement bulletins; inventory control; request processing; statistics gathering and analysis; the selective dissemination of information; the developing real-time loan and reservation system, etc.

The Bell Laboratories Library is in the process of developing an integrated system, named BELLMATIC, to provide (a) computer editing and production of announcement bulletins, (b) a personalized alerting service and (c) a wide range of logical search and retrieval operations. The primary input to the system will be up to 30,000 current technical papers scanned from selected journals and deeply indexed using a technical thesaurus developed to reflect Bell Laboratories' technical interests. The input mechanism is a typewriter coupled to an incremental tape recorder. The personalized alerting service will be coordinated with the announcement bulletin wherein the subject interests of the participants are to be matched against the descriptor sets for each announced item in order to direct the user's attention to items of interest to him.

Bibliographical References

1 Kennedy, R. A. Information handling and use at Bell Telephone Laboratories (Talk presented at the American Book Publishers Council, Conference on Information Science and Technology, New York, March 15, 1967).

2 Bell Telephone Laboratories. Description of MERCURY including the new psychology section of thesaurus (MERCURY Bulletin No. 2, January 15, 1967).

ESSO Research and Engineering Company, Linden, N. J.
Technical Information Division

The Technical Information Division (TID) of ESSO Research and Engineering Company is responsibile for organizing the flow of information into and within the Company and among its affiliates. To discharge its functions the TID is staffed with information scientists or information researchers, as they are called, who are qualified and competent as scientific people in other research divisions. These information researchers have the primary responsibility of seeing that all pertinent information, both current and past, from all available sources should not only reach the researcher's desk promptly but should also be analyzed and synthesized for convenient use. The information researchers, or other members of the group having special knowledge of information handling and literature searches, also guide the individual research scientists in making their own searches as required.

The functions of the Technical Information Division have been grouped under four major heads: Information acquisition, Information analysis, Information dissemination, and Information system research. The Company's technical library, which was established in 1919, is now part of the Technical Information Division. The library has over 50,000 volumes of books and bound periodicals, over 70,000 patents from the United States and other countries, and a large volume of published reports and preprints. The library also subscribes to about 600 technical journals. It is responsible for the acquisition, storage, technical processing, and dissemination of published literature to support the research activities of over 2,000 scientists and engineers engaged in research at ESSO and its affiliates. A separate Reports Collection Unit stores, indexes, and retrieves the Company generated research and engineering reports and memoranda.

The TID-generated technical abstracts bulletins, technical reports indexes and other bibliographic publications are prepared and edited by the information researchers.

In the petroleum industry there is a heavy dependence on the API Central Abstracting and Indexing Services which publishes the weekly API Abstracts of Refining Literature and API Abstracts of Refining Patents, covering the basic current literature and patents of Company interest on crudes and related raw materials, petroleum products and processes, chemical products and processes, highpolymer products and processes, specialty products, catalysts, analyses and tests, engineering, corrosion, pollution problems, safety and contributing sciences. The API also provides computer-based indexes to API literature and patent abstracts in the form of an alphabetical subject index, a dual-dictionary coordinate index, and computer search tapes for bibliographic control of petroleum literature. However, the Technical Information Division found it necessary to issue ESSO Technical Abstracts, a monthly bulletin, to supplement these API bulletins by covering additional journals, preprints, patents, and government reports in the petroleum and related areas. Another TID bulletin (semi-monthly) deals with EREC library acquistions and new company papers.

The Technical Information Division also publishes several sponsored abstracts bulletins which include the Transportation and Storage Bulletin (monthly), Iron and Steel Manufacturing Bulletin (monthly), Agricultural Chemicals (monthly) and Synthetic Fuels (monthly). The distribution of these bulletins is limited to the specialists who are engaged in research in these areas.

The monthly Technical Reports Index with a semi-annual cumulative index is the key to Company and affiliate reports that contain data from research and development programs in the fields of petroleum and chemical processes, products, and engineering. Each index contains a list of reports, an author index, and an alphabetical subject index.

The Technical Information Division computerized the information on research and engineering reports and memoranda generated in the Company in 1962 and the index to the literature and patents abstracted by the TID in 1964. The input cost of the Technical Reports Index with 30 indexing terms per document is $20.00 and the input cost of the abstract literature with 8 indexing terms per document is $3.00 ($18.00 including abstracting costs). The computer systems have also been used by the Library for journal ordering and routing. The equipment used are the Flexowriter punched tape-to-card converter and the IBM 7094 and IBM 1401 computers.

Eight years ago, at the Fifth World Petroleum Congress, W. T. Knox, then Director of the ESSO Technical Information Division, described the functions and activities of the information-research scientists and engineers in the ESSO Research and Engineering Company and concluded with the following words:

> Information-research activities have already demonstrated large returns, by virtue of stimulating closer attention to the published information, by uncovering valuable leads to new processes and products by developing new techniques for handling information, and by providing well-rounded, complete surveys of pertinent research areas. The excellent results thus far obtained through the use of information research scientists and engineers would appear to make this new technique worthy of serious consideration by all members of the petroleum industry. [1]

Bibliographical References

[1] Cloud, G. H. and Knox, W. T. "Information Research: a new tool for the petroleum industry" (Paper presented at the Fifth World Petroleum Congress, 1959).

Smith, Kline and French Laboratories, Philadelphia
Science Information Department

At the Smith, Kline and French Laboratories (SK&F) the handling of all scientific information is centralized in the Science Information Department, which reports to the R & D Division.

The Documentation Section of the Science Information Department handles the acquisition, storage, dissemination, and retrieval of the scientific literature. The other sections of the Department are the Biomedical Sciences, Physical Sciences, Statistical, and Product Surveillance Sections. Senior information scientists who are high level specialists in various subject disciplines, having almost the same order of scientific recognition as the laboratory and clinical scientists, are attached to these sections. These people join the research and development teams and shoulder the responsibility for critical evaluation and the creative use of information in furthering the teams' scientific activities. All the technical information, including experimental and clinical data accumulated on a project, is digested by information scientists in the research team in order to be communicated to, and interpreted for, other members of the team. In the Statistics Section of the Science Information Department, statisticians apply statistical techniques to research and development problems and guide the bench scientists in designing laboratory tests and clinical trials. They also help in evaluating test results. SK&F is the only company of its kind to centralize all biostatistical operations in the information group.

The Library, which is a unit under the Documentation Section, handles the acquisition and processing of books, journals, and other published material. It is also charged with responsibility for systematization and storage of the departmental files of the company.

A group of junior scientists with experience in information handling scan the current literature received in the Library for information pertaining to current research and development projects in which SK&F scientists are engaged. The material of specific interest to a research team is immediately passed on to the appropriate science section of the Science Information Department and the senior information scientist working in the group passes it on to the team members.

For communication of the current scientific literature of more general interest to the scientific community of the company, junior information scientists attached to the Documentation Section abstract and index such literature and it is issued in the <u>Weekly Literature Information Bulletin</u> for distribution throughout the company. The staff of the Documentation Section also makes retrospective literature searches on demand.

The Documentation Section is also responsible for the collection, analysis, and storage of the large volume of unpublished internal technical reports and clinical data generated in the company. The information in these reports and data files is coded and transferred to punched cards, or, in some cases, to computer tapes for quick machine scanning. Mechanization is limited to the handling of internally generated data and data from case reports submitted by investigators working with new drugs.

The punched card equipment is located in the Science Information Department and is used by its data processing group. The computer tapes are searched on the company's central computer.

The Science Information Department of SK&F has organized its information facilities so that it can play a vital role in planning and implementation of research and development work. It contributes at each stage of the research and development process by manipulating, interpreting and evaluating the needed information. The degree to which the senior information scientists participate in such functions is one of the outstanding features of the SK&F organization. The Science Information Department has access to a complete range of IBM data processing equipment, such as key punch, verifier, reproducing punch, card providing machine, IBM 407 accounting machine, and the IBM 101 electronic statistical machine, as well as the IBM 1401, IBM 1410, and LPC-30 computers.

Bibliographical References

1 Rockwell, Harriet E. *Information for Research and Development* (Science Information Department, Smith, Kline and French Laboratories, 1961).

Lockheed Missiles & Space Company, Sunnyvale, California
Technical Information Center

The library resources of the Technical Information Center of the LMSC, the largest in the aerospace industry, are organized into reports, books, and periodical collections to meet the research needs of approximately 11,050 scientists, engineers, and administrative personnel of the organization.

In the collection of reports, which forms the critical and vital source of scientific and technical information, there are over 400,000 technical reports, either generated by LMSC or by outside agencies, both governmental and private. These are in original form as well as in Defense Documentation Center (DDC) reproductions and NASA microfiches. The collection is growing at the rate of 60,000 items per year.

Complete collections of Department of Defense (DoD) generated or funded research reports in microfiche format, AEC-sponsored unclassified technical reports, and NASA unclassified reports, are available in neighboring libraries under certain conditions.

Literature searching:

The scientists, engineers, and other research personnel at LMSC do not normally involve themselves in literature searches, since these searches, can be done more economically and efficiently by the information specialists attached to the TIC. These information specialists, or literature searchers, as they are called, all have extensive experience in literature search techniques as well as in screening, reviewing, and synthesizing pertinent literature. The requesting scientist or engineer is provided with abstracts on standard 5 x 8 inch cards, with each citation giving enough information for the reader to determine whether he needs to read the full item. At the end of the search, the information specialist indexes the compiled abstracts and prepares an annotated bibliography for publication. These published bibliographies are sent to all Lockheed Technical Information Centers and are also distributed to major federal documentation centers. More than 500 annotated and indexed subject bibliographies have so far been generated by the TIC literature search personnel in direct support of research, development, and other specialized efforts of LMSC.

Information Retrieval

A system for applying computer operations to various information services is being developed at the LMSC Technical Information Center. The Machine Application to Technical Information Center Operations (MATICO) has been planned for implementation in stages; it will implement such advanced information retrieval concepts as selective dissemination of information, autoabstracting, and automatic literature search. During the past two years, a system has been developed for preparing catalog cards and a Key-Word-in-Context (KWIC) index to technical reports. In this phase of the operation, the titles of new publications are also generated on a separate tape that produces the Key-Word-in-Title listing. The MATICO system is compatible with those of NASA and other governmental information centers using magnetic tape for storage and retrieval. An on-line information retrieval system with a dialogue capability to assure accurate and rapid response to the question asked is under development.

Library Catalog in Microform

The computer-produced library catalog has 1,600,000 retrieval points to provide multiple access for quick identification of resources in the collection and for rapid dissemination and retrieval. It is the first of its kind in the United States. The catalog is arranged in six sections: source, title, author(s), contract number, subjects, and report numbers/call number. It is reproduced on 16 mm microfilm form, which compresses these 1.6 million retrieval points into 40 cartridges. Each cartridge contains 100 ft of film bearing 1,800 two-column pages of computerized catalog text produced by the SC 4020.

A complete, cumulated, and corrected microfilm catalog is produced quarterly. Computer processing time together with duplicate microfilm processing, label generation, cartridge loading, and distribution to the operating location takes ten work days.

Between periodic microfilm catalog production runs, users are kept informed of titles added to the collections by New Reports & Books, which is produced semi-monthly by a computer in KWIC format.

To minimize the queuing problems due to multiple simultaneous use of the catalog, multiple microfilm readers and catalog cartridges have been installed for library users. In addition, the cataloging staff in the library has two sets of microfilm cartridges and two readers and the literature searchers have been provided with one set of cartridges and one reader for independent use. The microfilm catalog is reported to be less costly than a computer-produced card catalog or a computer-produced book catalog.

The new microfilm catalog has been accepted both by the scientists and the library staff, including literature searchers attached to LMSC, as the system has demonstrated that it has reduced look-up time and is easy to operate. According to TIC, the microfilm system gives an annual net saving of $13,000 because (1) card filling costs are eliminated; (2) the cost of catalog cases is eliminated; and (3) there is a great saving in the space that would be required for a card catalog.

An additional advantage of the computer-produced microfilm catalog is that the printed book catalog could be produced at a much lower cost by using the microfilm master as the printing base. W. A. Kozumplik, in his article, "Computer-produced Microfilm Library Catalog,"[1] has worked out the comparative cost of the book catalog using the microfilm master and the copyflow process and using the computer printout and multilith. He estimated that the use of the microfilm catalog as the printing base would lower the printing costs of the book catalog by two-thirds.

The data processing and other equipment used at the LMSC Technical Information Center are the IBM 826, the IBM 7094, the Stromberg-Carlson 4020, the IBM 360/30, the IBM 360/50 and the Bell and Howell reader printer model 531.

Bibliographical References

1 Kozumplik, W. A. and Lange, R. T. "Computer-produced Microfilm Library Catalog" (<u>American Documentation</u> 18(2):67-80, April, 1967).

2 Lockheed Missiles and Space Company. Pamphlets on the Technical Information Center, and literature search.

IBM Advanced Systems Development Division, Los Gatos, California
Research Library

The small Research Library of the IBM Advanced Systems Development Division (ASDD) adds about 1,500 books and 3,000 reports annually to its collection, subscribing to approximately 650 current journals and servicing between 500 and 600 specialists attached to ASDD.

Through the efforts of the Librarian, Miss M. Griffin, all the major operations in the Library have been automated, using the computer configuration available at this research center. It is used for the processes involved in order work, preparation of the book for circulation, including the book label, circulation cards, catalog and other inventory for bibliographic control and dissemination. It is also used for serials control, including subscription, registration, routing, bindery information, and circulation. According to Miss Griffin, the computerized library system has reduced the amount of time required for acquisition and processing, has minimized errors in recording, has provided computer assistance in indexing, has brought about faster retrieval of information, and in general has brought the Library closer to the readers. This totally automated library system is based on the IBM Administrative Terminal System (ATS) and is typewriter-linked to an IBM 1460 data processing system for bibliographic input, an IBM 7090 computer for processing and sorting, and an IBM 1401 computer for output. The computer time allotted for library operations is about 30 minutes each working day. The reason for using such a variety of systems is that all this equipment is available at ASDD.

The Library is engaged in developing systems on an IBM 360 for real-time bibliographic searching, using an IBM 2260 display station in which the user will enter his request in natural language, and is also developing systems for batch searching for comprehensive bibliographies. All the record keeping now being processed on a variety of data processing systems will be converted to the IBM 360 when it is in operation.

The system design and the mechanized operations in the Library have been detailed in a manual[1] to serve as a helpful guide to other librarians.

Bibliographical References

1 International Business Machines <u>Mechanized Library Procedures for the IBM Advanced Systems Development Division Library,</u> Los Gatos, California (International Business Machines Corp., 1967).

IBM, Thomas J. Watson Research Center, Yorktown Heights, New York
Research Library

This Research Library has a collection of about 25,000 books, 15,000 volumes of bound journals, and subscribes to 1,000 current journals. It serves approximately 1,100 research scientists and technologists attached to this IBM Center.

The Library started the mechanization of some of its routine operations in 1962 based on a single-card record keeping system for its book collection. The punched card record initiated at the time of acquisition is subsequently verified and modified when the item is in the process of being cataloged. This unit record on a punched card is manipulated by tabulating card machines or by an IBM 1401 computer to produce a processing information list (PIL),[1] the circulation charge card, the book pocket label, the shelflist printout, and a main entry index to the shelflist.

In the circulation control system, the circulation charge card, which is a by-product of the computer-based shelflist card, is used to produce basic loan records-- a record of all books on loan arranged by author, a record of all books on loan arranged by borrower, as well as overdue and recall notices. The records are updated once a week using the computer, and a high speed 1403 printer is used to print the overdue notices at the rate of 600 lines per minute.

For serials control, the automated unit card record is manipulated to provide subscription, binding and printed lists of holdings.

The Library uses punched card data processing machines (Sorter, Tabulator, Collator) and the IBM 1401 computer. The computer is used approximately 3 1/2 hours per week for library operations. According to G. E. Randall, Manager of the Research Library, the use of machines in library operations has considerably increased the accuracy of library records. Thus, library service is more efficient and, at the same time, costs are kept down.

Bibliographical References

1 Randall, G. E. and Bristol, R. P. "PIL (Processing Information List) or A Computer-controlled Processing Record" (Special Libraries, February, 1964, p. 82-86).

2 Randall, G. E. and Gibson, R. W. "Circulation Control by Computer" (Special Libraries, July-August, 1963, p. 333-338).

3 Randall, G. E. "Unit Record System for Serial Control in a Special Library" (IBM Library Mechanization Symposium. Endicott, N. Y., May 25-27, 1964).

IBM Technical Information Retrieval Center

The IBM Technical Information Retrieval Center (ITIRC) located at Yorktown Heights, N. Y., has been operating since 1964 as the central information retrieval and dissemination center for the IBM community all over the world. The ITIRC system is closely linked to more than 40 IBM libraries and over 75 percent of the users of the Current Information Selection Service (CIS) have access to one or more of these libraries. Teleprocessing techniques have been used to link these libraries and make the information retrieval service as effective and current as possible.

At ITIRC, besides literature searching both current and retrospective document announcement bulletins, and micro-processing, one of the major activities of the Center is the current awareness system known as Current Information Selection (CIS) service.

IBM developed the normal text information retrieval system as a result of several years of research and experimentation. The ITIRC implemented this sophisticated system with a successful CIS to disseminate scientific information to approximately 2,400 IBM scientists and engineers within and outside the United States.

In the information transfer operations, an abstract of 200 to 300 words, all relevant bibliographic data (which include author, title, publishing source, and source codes), and assigned subject index terms of all the documents analyzed in the Center are reproduced in normal text, in upper and lower case format, on magnetic tape. The thesaurus for assigning subject terms contains 8,000 major entries and 20,000 to 30,000 cross-references.

The user profiles and search questions, which are usually

phrased by the scientists in normal English, are converted to machine-readable form by the information specialists in the Center, using the appropriate contextual logic with the necessary words and phrases. In the search system up to 100 retrospective questions are searched in six minutes per tape using the IBM 7090 computer, which prints out the answer. A report is mailed to the requester with an evaluation response card.

In the Current Information Selection service, the individual profiles are matched four times a month against data on current literature which covers IBM documents, IBM invention disclosures, non-IBM documents, and current journals. The abstracts that match the profiles are printed out and promptly mailed to the individuals with an evaluation response card for information and use.

The CIS users normally obtain the IBM reports in which they are interested from their local IBM Library. On request, the ITIRC also provides, in microfiche copies or hard copies, documents which are not covered by copyright.

Between 1,500 and 2,000 new documents are put into the ITIRC information system each month. In 1966 over 500,000 abstracts were sent out to an average of 1,400 users. The input was 12,500 documents. The average user received abstracts of 3 percent of the total documents recorded and announced during the year. The users rated 83 percent of the notifications as relevant to their interest. The database tape is also used for printing special bulletins and library tools (circulation control cards, cumulative indexes, and source code lists) for use in the IBM Technical Libraries in the United States and Europe. ITIRC initially used IBM 7090-1401 computers for information handling. Recently the system has been reprogrammed in the IBM 360 computer, which provides remote inquiry and real-time capabilities. The information specialists and data-processing technicians in the Center are actively engaged in research on hardware and software to improve the systems, using the latest developments in computer technology.

Bibliographical References

1 Magnino, Joseph J. IBM Technical Information Center Retrieval: Progress and plans (Report submitted at the Annual Convention of the American Documentation Institute, October, 1966).

2 Nelson, Paul J. User Profiling for Normal Text Retrieval (paper submitted at the Annual Convention of the American Documentation Institute, October, 1967).

National Aeronautics and Space Administration
Scientific and Technical Information System

The National Aeronautics and Space Administration (NASA) is charged with the responsibility for providing comprehensive bibliographical services covering world literature on aerospace science, by a Federal Act of July, 1958. The information services of NASA are handled by two establishments: (1) NASA Scientific and Technical Information Facility, managed by Documentation Incorporated, a private organization which has been operating under the direction of NASA's Scientific and Technical Information Division since 1962 on contract basis; and (2) the American Institute of Aeronautics and Astronautics (AIAA) whose services have been partly supported by NASA since 1963. These two organizations work in very close collaboration but the areas of work do not overlap.

The NASA Scientific and Technical Information Facility acquires and analyzes the domestic and foreign technical reports and memoranda covering aerospace subjects and prepares two semi-monthly abstracting journals--Scientific and Technical Aerospace Reports (STAR) and CSTAR in which classified or restricted reports are announced. The American Institute of Aeronautics and Astronautics (AIAA) processes the published journal literature on the subject and prepares a third semi-monthly abstracting journal, International Aerospace Abstracts (IAA). The abstracts and indexing worksheets of IAA are sent on to NASA, so that thereafter all processing can be monitored by the same facilities and equipment. The two complementary journals--STAR and IAA, published on alternate weeks, provide comprehensive access to the world's current literature on aerospace science, and technology. STAR contains over 30,000 abstracts of technical reports, memoranda, etc., per year, and the IAA lists over 20,000 abstracts of printed journal literature annually.

The abstracts are mostly informative and are normally limited to 150 words.

When author abstracts or abstracts generated at other centers are not readily available, abstracts are prepared by subject specialists.

STAR and IAA both use the same 34 subject categories. These cover 8 disciplines, 18 different areas of engineering, and 2 interdisciplinary subjects. The categories were developed after thorough analysis of the subjects by STAR and IAA, in consultation with the subject specialists.

A new technique developed in STAR and IAA is the use of an expanded title, called "Notation of Content," containing several words consistent with the system's indexing vocabulary. The Notation of Content is used to feed the computer indexing process, known as SWIFT (Selected Word in Full Title), to give more dependable access than an index derived from the uncontrolled original title.

For efficient retrieval, both the publications STAR and IAA are provided with all possible indexes: (1) subject, (2) corporate author or source, (3) personal author, (4) contract number--in cumulative indexes only, (5) report/accession number, and (6) accession/report number. In IAA, which deals with printed literature, the same indexes are provided except that a simple accession number index is used in place of the accession/report number and report/accession number indexes, and the corporate author and contract number indexes are omitted.

In the printed publications, the indexes are composite terms, phrases, or pre-coordinated terms rather than single words or uniterms. On an average, five such terms are assigned to each title. The indexer also assigns a number of indexing terms that are single words, unbound terms, or uniterms, which do not appear in the published index. These terms, called "machine terms," are stored on NASA's magnetic tapes with other descriptive catalog information for machine retrieval in depth. On an average, fifteen such terms are developed for each document. The vocabulary used for subject indexing, both for published and machine terms, and the cross-references used in STAR cumulative indexes, are directly monitored by the Information Division. STAR uses approximately 18,000 separate subject terms for indexing.

STAR, besides being used as a bibliographic tool for current awareness and search, is helpful for retrospective searching and for prompt issuance of the cumulative indexes. The cumulative indexes are prepared and distributed, with a time lag of two to three weeks, at the end of each quarter.

The NASA also publishes special and continuing bibliographies in areas of special interest to provide for more extensive retrospective searches in these areas. Approximately 500 bibliographies and literature searches are prepared annually. These bibliographies are periodically updated by supplements.

In addition to STAR, and a classified series of STAR, the NASA Facility issues six other publications: (1) Technical Report, (2) Technical Notes, (3) Technical Memorandums, (4) Contractor Reports, (5) Technical Translations, and (6) Special Publications. NASA also puts out four publications which report on technical innovations that may interest industries and technologists. These are: (1) Tech Briefs, (2) Technology Utilization Notes, (3) Technology Utilization Reports, and (4) Technology Survey.

NASA is one of the first organizations in the United States to use microfiche for the storage and dissemination of technical literature. The microcopying system provides microfiche copies of each document abstracted and announced in STAR as well as for the documents in IAA which are not limited by copyright. Microfiche copies of report literature are regularly distributed to approximately 4,000 recipients in NASA research centers and contractor organizations, to 200 universities and large public libraries, to 550 foreign government agencies and institutions, and to 5,000 industrial establishments.

The bibliographic information generated at the NASA Scientific and Technical Information Facility and the American Institute of Aeronautics and Astronautics, stored on magnetic tapes, constitutes a comprehensive, updated, and readily accessible data base to provide a variety of information services, including cumulative indexes, retrospective searches, and the Selective Dissemination of Information (SDI) programs. Over 1,000 scientists and technologists in the various NASA laboratories subscribe to the SDI Service. The returns from the SDI recipients are systematically analyzed and evaluated to find the effectiveness of the individual profile and the degree of matching obtained in such service.

The computer system operating at the NASA Facility consists of the IBM 1410 linear file search system and the IBM 1401 model II computer. The linear search system improved the capability to produce bibliographies and compilations of file data of all sorts. Photon and GRACE (Graphic Arts Composition Equipment) are used for composition of the printed bibliographies and other publications. Besides the computer printouts, the NASA Facility distributes magnetic tapes containing bibliographic data, together with the computer programs, to serve as the basic data input to several independent systems. About 30 organizations, which include all NASA research centers, a number of major NASA contractors, and several universities, use the NASA data base tapes to organize decentralized services. The tapes are updated twice each month. The search system and the bibliographic services provided by NASA are under continuous evaluation to guide further improvement of the service.

NASA provides one of the most dynamic information handling agencies of the federal government. The information scientists attached to the Facility are continually researching on information transfer problems with the aim of improving services.

Bibliographical References

1 Brandhorst, W. T. and Eckert, F. "NASA Search System Analysis Sheet" (American Documentation 16(2):124-126, April, 1965).

2 Eckert, P. F. Development and Operation of Machine Search Systems at NASA's Scientific and Technical Information Facility, Presented at the 150th meeting of the American Chemical Society, Division of Chemical Literature, Atlantic City, N. J., September, 1965.

3 Brandhorst, W. T. and Eckert, P. F. The Guide to the Processing, Storage and Retrieval of Bibliographic Information at the NASA Scientific and Technical Information Facility. National Aeronautics and Space Administration, (NASA, CR-62033), July, 1966.

4 SLA Government Information Service Committee "Users Look at Information Centers" (Special Libraries 57(1):45-49, January, 1966).

National Library of Medicine
MEDLARS Information Systems Division

The National Library of Medicine (NLM) originated in 1836 as the Library of the Surgeon General's Office, United States Army. This library, now one of the three national libraries of the United States, is probably the largest medical library in the world. Since 1879, the library has published comprehensive subject indexes to disseminate literature on the biomedical sciences to medical scientists and practitioners engaged in research and investigation.

To handle the ever increasing literature output and to speed up the indexing and processing of bibliographic information, NLM developed a plan for a computer-based information storage and retrieval system called MEDLARS (Medical Literature Analysis and Retrieval System) in 1961. It took three years of work on the system design, study of work flow, computer programming, system testing and other preliminaries before the MEDLARS system could be fully commissioned in January, 1964, to function as a national biomedical information system. The MEDLARS tape file contains citations to biomedical journal articles published since that date (January, 1964). Dr. Cummings, Director of the National Library of Medicine, at a seminar on Electronic Information Handling held at Pittsburg University in 1963, stated the objectives of MEDLARS as follows:

> First, the rapid dissemination of lists of current publications in the medical field, including the monthly publication, Index Medicus, and other regular recurring bibliographies in more specialized areas such as cancer and heart disease. Second, the bibliographic control of the medical periodical literature available for rapid retrieval in response to subject-oriented queries of our computer files. We call such searches demand bibliographies. Third, the wide availability of the MEDLARS data base to other libraries and research institutions which may duplicate the retrieval capacity of this system and make more specialized use of the contents of the file within their own research programs.

MEDLARS is the only library-based computerized system now in operation for the retrieval of references to published biomedical literature. To fulfill its objectives, the system operates in three major subdivisions: an input subsystem, a retrieval subsystem, and a publication subsystem.

In the input subsystem, professional librarians and literature analysts with strong subject backgrounds scan the medical periodicals, analyze the subject content of each article, and assign appropriate subject headings to it from the Library's controlled vocabulary "Medical Subject Headings" (MeSH) which lists approximately 6,400 terms. On an average, eight subject headings are assigned to each article for printing in Index Medicus. Up to thirty-two additional subject headings are assigned for storage on the computer system for searches in depth. The bibliographic details and the descriptors assigned to each article are punched on paper tape by Flexowriters, then edited and transferred to magnetic tape for incorporation into the "Processed Citation" and "Compressed Citation" data files. The Processed Citation File contains citations for publishing Index Medicus and other recurring bibliographies issued as serial publications. The Compressed Citation File contains citations in depth needed for retrieval of answers to complex reference questions and for compilation of demand bibliographies on highly specific subjects. Currently, 180,000 articles from 2,400 medical journals are processed annually and stored in the computer system; this number is expected to rise to 250,000 articles from 3,000 current journals by 1969. Language experts provide English translations of foreign articles, which are written in 40 different languages and cover a high percentage of the significant literature.

In the retrieval subsystem the search specialists, having extensive training both in indexing and in the logic of computer searching, analyze the requests for bibliographic citations, detail the relevant search elements, and formulate search statements intelligible to the computer system. Formulated search requests are punched into paper tape, edited, and batched for computer processing. The retrieved citations are recorded on magnetic tape and are then printed out in natural language. Demand bibliographies are normally printed on the computer's high speed printer.

In the publication subsystem Index Medicus, Bibliography of

Medical Reviews, and similar recurring bibliographies, are processed for printing from photopositive film. The Honeywell computer-produced magnetic tapes of the Processed Citation File are used for preparation of repro film by a computer driven typesetter, GRACE (Graphic Art Composing Equipment). GRACE converts digital information from the magnetic tape to high quality typography and operates at a speed of about 300 characters per second. It provides 226 different characters, and can produce 23 cm wide positive photographic film or paper. The film masters are used for plate-making, printing, and publication. With the use of GRACE the composing time of each issue of Index Medicus has been reduced from 25 days to 16 hours.

Besides Index Medicus and Bibliography of Medical Reviews, published by the National Library of Medicine, a number of other bibliographic periodicals are issued for the benefit of different institutions using MEDLARS tape. Cerebro-Vascular Bibliography, published for the National Institute of Neurological Diseases and Blindness and the National Heart Institute; Index to Rheumatology, for the American Rheumatism Association, and; Index to Dental Literature, produced for the American Dental Association and the National Institute of Dental Research, are some of these publications.

With a view to decentralizing the MEDLARS search and retrieval capability for wider and more prompt dissemination of medical literature, the National Library of Medicine is making duplicate tapes available to several other libraries for use on local computer configurations. The tapes are updated periodically from the MEDLARS master tapes. The Biomedical Library of the University of California (Los Angeles), the University of Colorado Medical Center (Denver), the University of Alabama Medical Center (Birmingham), the University of Michigan (Ann Arbor), and Harvard University (Boston) are operating as MEDLARS decentralized search centers.

Requests for sharing the MEDLARS' searching capabilities have already been received from more than forty university medical centers, government agencies, and private organizations and the Library is attempting to develop a regional network of MEDLARS Centers to provide rapid access to the world's biomedical literature.

To improve the analysis, indexing, and exhaustive search of increasing biomedical literature, the specialists in medical literature and indexing methods are continually formulating and revising subject headings. A group of highly qualified scientists is working to develop research-oriented descriptors to meet the growing interdisciplinary needs in medical research. This controlled vocabulary, "Medical Subject Headings," is not only the key to the retrieval of information for recurring and demand bibliographies of the National Library of Medicine, but can also be used as subject headings for cataloging books and other printed literature in this library as well as in several other medical libraries.

A team of system specialists is engaged in research to improve the MEDLARS System, using more sophisticated hardware and software, and is also trying to develop systems to mechanize some of the routine operations in the Library, such as acquisition, cataloging, and serials record. The cataloging service will eventually produce catalog cards for use by other libraries and will issue printed book catalogs each year and a cumulated catalog every five years. Projects are also in hand to study the feasibility of on-line indexing and citation output, development of drug information modules, and storage and retrieval of graphic images.

The MEDLARS system now uses Honeywell 800 and Honeywell H-200 computers, the Photon 900 typesetter, the computer-activated optical printer called GRACE (Graphic Arts Composing Equipment), Friden Flexowriters and IBM keypunches and verifiers.

Bibliographical References

1 Austin, Charles, J. "The MEDLARS System" (Datamation 10(2): 28-31, December, 1964).

2 Karel, Leonard, Charles J. Austin, and Martin M. Cummings "Computerized Bibliographic Services for Biomedicine." Science 148(3671): 766-772, May 7, 1965.

3 The Medlars Story at the National Library of Medicine, Washington, D. C., U. S. Department of Health, Education, and Welfare, Public Health Service, 1963, reprinted 1965, p. 74.

Institute for Scientific Information, Philadelphia

The Institute for Scientific Information (ISI), established in the late 1950's, is one of the largest information centers in the United States handling scientific information services on a commercial basis. A large number of information scientists with strong backgrounds in science subjects, librarians, system analysts, and data processing technicians are engaged in ISI's retrieval and dissemination activities. Over 1,600 important journals on science and technology are analyzed and processed to provide a number of computer-based literature searching services, plus weekly services of a simpler nature such as Current Contents, Chemical Sciences; Current Contents, Physical Sciences and Current Contents, Life Sciences. The Current Contents series has been well received by the scientific community and it is estimated that over 60,000 scientists use these media for current awareness.

The computer-based abstracting and indexing service Index Chemicus, begun in 1960, reports about 120,000 newly synthesized chemicals each year. It is estimated that more than 10,000 synthetic chemists, pharmacologists, and other scientists throughout the world use the weekly Index Chemicus for information on chemical literature.

The Science Citation Index, a comprehensive multi-disciplinary index to science, is a unique service developed at ISI. Dr. Eugene Garfield described the Citation Index as "an ordered list of cited articles each of which is accompanied by a list of citing articles. The citing article is identified by a source citation, the cited article by a reference citation. The index is arranged by reference citations."[1] The concept of citation indexing is the result of several years of research by Dr. Garfield and his associates at the center.

Another computer-generated bibliographical index provided by the ISI is Permuterm Subject Index, which is integrated with major ISI computer-based services, including the Science Citation Index. It is also integrated with the ISI Magnetic Tapes, the ISI Search Services, and the ASCA III Services. The Permuterm Subject Index needs to be used in conjunction with Source Index, the companion volume of Science Citation Index. The 1966 Permutern Subject Index recorded approximately 250,000 articles, indexed under an average of 35 permuted pairs of terms, from 1,600 basic journals on science and technology. Since 1965, the ISI has been providing to individual scientists as a personal service, computer-based selective disseminations of information, which goes by the name of "Automatic Subject Citation Alert" (ASCA) and is also based on the citation indexing principle.

ISI also provides some of its services on subscribers' magnetic tapes. Several information centers attached to research establishments and industries find it more economical to request such comprehensive data on tapes and to run the tapes at local computer centers for more specific searches, listing, and selective dissemination purposes. On the ISI citation tapes approximately 64,000 cited references from nearly 5,400 current items are processed and delivered on subscribers' tapes at weekly intervals. In 1967, more than 3,000,000 references, cited by approximately 275,000 source items in 1,600 scientific periodicals, have been stored on magnetic tapes.

Another service on a yearly subscription basis is the "source tapes." Approximately 5,400 current items are transferred and delivered on subscribers' tapes at weekly intervals; complete files covering more than 775,000 source items from the scientific literature published from 1964 to 1966 are also available in annual cumulation.

ISI does not limit its service to the processed information; it provides copies of the articles on demand. To fulfill this responsibility ISI operates the Original Articles Tear Sheet Service (OATS), for which multiple copies of journals are procured and stored in ISI, to provide pages of the required article or articles on demand. This service ensures availability of specific literature without much trouble or delay and without photocopying.

The information scientists and technologists attached to ISI are actively engaged in continuing research on information handling problems and data processing in order to provide better and more economical services.

Bibliographical References

1 Garfield, E. "Science Citation Index: a new dimension in indexing" (Science 144(3619):649-54, May, 1964).

Washington University School of Medicine
Library

The Library of the School of Medicine, Washington University, St. Louis, under the able management of Dr. Estell Brodman and her associates, has gone through many changes during the last seven years to provide improved service to students, researchers in medical science, and the St. Louis medical community in general.

The Library has about 100,000 volumes, of which 60 percent are volumes of serials, and several thousand reprints and research reports. It receives over 1,500 current journals.

The quinquennial (1961/62 to 1965/66) review of the Library shows a 635 percent increase in the use of reading materials within the Library, a 112 percent increase in demand for interlibrary loans from other libraries, a 572 percent increase in literature searches, a 452 percent increase in the number of bibliographies compiled, and a 789 percent increase in the number of Xerox copies made, with only a 13.5 percent increase in staff. These data reflect not only the increased use of the Library, but also testify to the efficiency of the present operations. In the process of reorganization, the Library changed from the Dewey Decimal System to the National Library of Medicine classification scheme.

On the operational side, the Library changed from the manual record keeping to computers for circulation records, serial records, and acquisition and catalog records. The results of the Library's experiments on machine methods and the cost analysis, published in a series of articles in the Bulletin of the Medical Library Association from 1963 to 1966, provide useful data and serve as a guide for the automation of routine operations in small and medium-sized libraries.

The Library changed circulation control to machine methods, including computer-produced overdue notices and other listings. The Serials Section put all its records of periodical holdings onto punched cards for conversion onto magnetic tapes. This single input on punched cards is manipulated in a variety of ways to produce PHILSOM (Periodical Holdings in the library of the School of Medicine), periodic announcement lists, a catalog updating PHILSOM, arranged under title and subject, and other records for administrative control of the serials.

As an experiment on machine methods, the Library prepared a computer-generated printed book catalog for books added to the Library during the first nine months of 1965. The catalog was produced on the IBM 1401-1403 and 7072 which were available at the computer center of Washington University. In the preface of the catalog, Dr. Brodman recorded two major findings on this experimental book catalog--one on the readers' reactions and another on the printing costs. She says:

> The scientists at this Medical Center have shown no desire to have a library catalog at their finger-tips, just as readers in the nineteenth century public and even scholarly libraries refused to purchase catalogs of those collections. The Washington University School of Medicine Library has provided free copies of its semi-annual cumulated serial holdings lists... to all departments of the Medical Center for almost 3 years now, and has offered (by signs on bulletin boards) free copies of these lists to any registered reader who has need of them. The response has been deafening by its silence, and the number of copies of these records we produce has therefore steadily diminished. We do not believe a book catalog will be any more desired by our readers.
>
> The printed catalog runs close to 300 pages, or would be close to 250 pages had we photo-reduced it the usual 40 percent. Just printing and binding it, once we had the offset masters produced by the computer, cost about $600 for 200 copies. Were we to print such a catalog each year at our present rate of growth, we would need to budget $800 yearly. But it is unthinkable that we should not wish to cumulate the list. This means that the second year our printed catalog would cost about $1,600, the third year $2,400 and so on in arithmetic progression for as long as we wish to cumulate.
>
> If, however, we printed our catalog annually, whether cumulated or not, we would need to have supplementary catalogs for material added since the publication of the last catalog--whereupon we would be back to the problems encountered by nineteenth century libraries issuing

book catalogs.

These findings may help small and medium-sized libraries to make decisions about computer-generated catalogs in printed form. The manipulation and updating of the catalog from a single input in the computer is claimed to be efficient and economical, but the printing of the book catalog from the computer-generated printouts is said to be expensive.

The Library reprogrammed the acquisitions-cataloging system to take advantage of the University's recently installed IBM 360/50 computer with upper and lower case print chain capability and decided to bring out another experimental printed catalog of books covering all additions to the Library from January, 1965 to February, 1967. The cost of computer time for the updating and manipulation of the catalog data from computer storage for preparation of this second catalog came to $230.00 and the cost of printing and binding came to $1,730.00. It has now been decided to generate the computer-based catalogs quarterly and cumulate them annually. The printing of the catalog in book form was to be determined by demand and costs.

In addition to routine operations, the Library, in 1964, introduced computer-based indexing of personal files, such as published and unpublished reports, and the data and correspondence of scientists. In September, 1965, the Library began a current awareness service for faculty members and researchers at the Medical Center, combining two kinds of information: (1) the results of scanning current literature received in the Library, and (2) information obtained in the weekly service ASCA (Automatic Subject Citation Alertness), received from the Institute of Scientific Information on a subscription basis.

The Library is now engaged in developing systems to use MEDLARS tape when it was made available by the National Library of Medicine.

Bibliographical References

1 Pizer, I. H., Franz, D. R., and Brodman, E. "Mechanization of Library procedures in the medium-sized medical library: I. The serial record." Bulletin of the Medical Library Association 53:313-

338, July 1963.

2 Pizer, I. H., Anderson, I. T., and Brodman, E. "Mechanization of library procedures in the medium-sized medical library: II. Circulation records." ibid., 52:370-385, April, 1964.

3 Moore, E. A., Brodman, E. and Cohen, G. "Mechanization of library procedures in the medium-sized medical library: III. Acquisitions and cataloging." Bull. Med. Lib. A., 53:305-328, July 1965; also ibid., 54:259-260, July, 1966.

The John Crerar Library

The John Crerar Library, established in 1895, to serve the scientists and technologists throughout the United States was the only public library devoted exclusively to science and technology. In 1962, the Illinois Institute of Technology placed its library under the management of the Crerar Library when the Crerar Library moved to its new building on the campus of that institute. The library, now a combination public, academic, and special library, is considered one of the major scientific libraries in the world. The library collection of over one million volumes, includes 13,000 current periodicals, over 125,000 scientific translations from foreign languages collected as depository of the SLA Translation Center, and a large number of technical reports received as one of the Federal Regional Technical Reports Centers. It contains the basic resources to serve students, teachers, and researchers in scientific institutions and industrial establishments.

The Crerar Library recognized the need for special services to support increased industrial research and development, and established its Research Information Service (RIS) in 1947. The major activities of the Research Information Service include literature searches for current awareness service, preparation of abstracting and indexing bulletins, critical evaluation of the literature, compilation of subject bibliographies, and translation of foreign technical literature.

Scientists with high academic qualifications, working as literature searchers in the RIS group, scan over 13,500 periodicals and other serials received in the Crerar Library for the current awareness services. Instead of organizing current alerting or personalized services independently, a number of industrial and research establishments have entered into an agreement with the Crerar Library for such services on a cost basis. Two of the major abstracting bulletins compiled and issued by the RIS are Crerar Metal Abstracts and Leukemia Abstracts. The first one disseminates current information on certain metals of importance to industrial companies. The latter, supported by the Lenore Schwartz Leukemia Research Foundation, aims to provide free current awareness service to institutions and individuals engaged in research on leukemia.

The RIS staff also provides critical evaluation of the literature on specific subjects for preparation of reviews and subject bibliographies on demand. The language experts on the RIS staff provide English translations of scientific literature in foreign languages when needed. The translation service is supplemented by the large collection of translated documents of the SLA Translation Center managed by the Crerar Library since 1953. The Translation Center, a depository and information center for unpublished translations now has in its collection over 125,000 translations of scientific literature.

Crerar Library in cooperation with the Computer Center at the Illinois Institute of Technology has recently computerized the bibliographic data on translations for preparation of a published index arranged by COSATI subject categories. Since June, 1967 a computer-based semi-monthly publication, Translation Register-Index, has been issued on behalf of the SLA Translation Center.

Photocopying service is another major activity in the Crerar Library. A variety of photocopy services is offered to the scientific and industrial community at reasonable charges.

The Crerar Library, though very large and having a variety of library and information services, has no immediate plans to mechanize its functions. A system analyst, however, has been working as part of the library staff since 1966 to study the flow of work and cost analysis of various operations in the Library. The studies may help in the long run to devise systems for mechanizing the Library's routine operations and record keeping where found to be more efficient and more economical.

Both Dr. Herman H. Henkel, Executive Director, and Mr. William S. Budington, Librarian, believe that in special library service although machines can do part of the work, human judgement is vital.

Library of Congress
Automation Program

The largest library automation project now underway in the United States is the mechanization of the major bibliographic operations in the Library of Congress. In April, 1961, the Council of Library Resources, Inc. granted $100,000 for

> ...a survey of automating the organization, storage and retrieval of information in a large research library ... not only from the point of view of the functioning of an individual institution but also from that of a research library whose activities are inter-related with those of other research libraries.

Dr. Gilbert W. King headed a team of technical specialists appointed for undertaking this survey on the basis of operational data and cost of major bibliographic functions in the Library of Congress. The team of experts studied all the problems involved in the automation of library services and in the report Automation and the Library of Congress[1] recommended that certain functions of the Library be mechanized by 1972 to ensure improved bibliographic service to the nation.

The team also studied the economic feasibility of such an automation program, including the estimated cost of hardware and software of the system, salaries, and the maintenance of projected automated services. The costs of the current manual system projected in 1972 were used as basic cost data for comparison. The initial cost to secure system specifications and the conversion of files to machine-readable form was estimated at about $31.6 million. The annual operating cost was estimated at around $4.5 million which is $0.5 million less than the expenditures they projected for the manual system in 1972. On this point, the study team concluded that "even if the costs were the same, the benefits are demonstrably greater in the automated system, since it would provide a wide variety of new services and a greater refinement of existing services."

The King report reached the following general conclusions:

1. Automation can, within the next decade, augment and accelerate the services rendered by large research libraries and can have a profound effect upon their responsiveness to the needs of library users.

2. Automation of bibliographic processing, catalog searching and document retrieval is technically and economically feasible in large research libraries.

3. The retrieval of the intellectual content of books by automatic methods is not now feasible for large collections, but progress in that direction will be advanced by effective automation of cataloging and indexing functions.

4. Automation will enhance the adaptability of libraries to changes in the national research environment and will facilitate the development of a national library system.

5. Automation will reduce the cost-to-performance ratio; however, the Library should aim at the expansion of services rather than the reduction of total operating costs.

Both librarians and scientists in the United States received the King report with great enthusiasm. A conference was held at the Airle Foundation,[2] and several other seminars and symposia were held to discuss the findings of the report. Library experts and systems analysts published their reviews and comments in contemporary library journals.

As a first step to an automation program, the Library of Congress established its Information Systems Office (ISO) with the responsibility of developing a computer system for automation of bibliographic services in seven phases which are as follows: (1) survey of the present manual system, (2) system-requirements analysis, (3) functional description of a recommended system, (4) system specifications for equipment and procedures, (5) system design, (6) implementation of a new system, and (7) operation of the new system.

In 1965, the Information Systems Office made a detailed study of the existing manual operations in the Library of Congress with a view to providing descriptions of all such operations as well as to provide flow charts and other operational data needed to initiate a contract for an automated system. ISO recommended that 15 general areas or processing operations (out of 33 subsystems in the Library of Congress) and 12 major files, which in one way or other represent the catalog and known holdings of the Library, should be converted to machine readable form to complete the mechanization of the central bibliographic service.

To be more specific, the following areas of the central bibliographic system are under investigation for automation: (1) the order and exchange acquisition activities; (2) cataloging--both descriptive and subject; (3) recording serial receipts and controlling serial records; (4) controlling the binding records in so far as they relate to the bibliographic system; (5) circulation control, including both inventory control of material in the Library and that loaned outside; (6) processing control, i.e., providing controls for monitoring and locating materials in process and not fully under bibliographic control, and (7) provision of outputs to meet the needs of the Library's bibliographic program.[4]

As a part of the total automation of the central bibliographic system of the Library of Congress, the Information Systems Office is engaged in developing techniques for computer manipulation of the card catalog into machine-readable form. Much work has already been done in reevaluating the information which needs to be included in a catalog entry and in designing a suitable format for a machine readable catalog entry. The pilot project MARC[5] (Machine-Readable Catalog) to test the suitability of the format and feasibility of distributing catalog data in machine-readable form, began in November, 1966 to distribute weekly data base tape to sixteen participating libraries selected for experimental work.

The participating libraries use local computer facilities for manipulation of the tape to produce catalog cards, book catalogs, reading lists, etc., on an experimental basis, and then report on their experience, which will serve as a guide for necessary improvements. MARC will continue to be an experimental project until the extensions and modifications are completed. The Library of Congress, however, was expected to be ready by July, 1968 to sell machine-readable records to interested libraries through its Card Division.

It is expected that before long the Library of Congress will distribute machine-readable catalog data to the entire library community on a fee basis, similar to the present printed card distribution program.

A number of other projects related to the total automation program are either in progress or in the planning stage. The ISO staff is working jointly with the Processing Department to analyze the subject headings used by the Library from the viewpoint of their suitability for machine processing. The LC subject headings have been converted to machine-readable form. This was used to print the 7th edition of the List of Subject Headings. Another project is the analysis of the structure of subject headings and of filing rules to find out what changes are necessary for computer manipulation of catalog records. Both the projects are prerequisite to computer-based bibliographies, book catalogs, and other printed listings.

It is hoped that the automation of the bibliographic system of the Library of Congress will lead to a computer-based library network, linking libraries throughout the country to the Library of Congress.

Barbara Markuson in a recent paper reported on the developmental work in automation at the Library of Congress and remarked:

> Many of the developments which may result from the LC system study may be transferable to other libraries, but many smaller libraries will find these too sophisticated or too costly to use directly... The experiences within the Library of Congress and in the field, however, should contribute to an increased understanding of the role automation will play during the next few decades. [6]

Bibliographical References

1 King, Gilbert W. (ed.) Automation and the Library of Congress (Washington, D.C., Library of Congress, 1963).

2 Markuson, Barbara E. (ed.) Libraries and Automation: Proceedings of the Conference on Libraries and Automation held at Airle Foundation, Warrenton, Virginia, May 26-30, 1963. Washington, D.C., Library of Congress, 1964.

3 Automation and the Library of Congress: three views by Robert M. Hayes, Ralph H. Parker and Gilbert W. King; "Dialogues with a Catalog" by Don R. Swanson; "The Systems Approach to Library Planning" by Merrill M. Flood; "The Development of a Methodology for System Design and its Role in Library Education" by Robert M. Hayes; "Theoretical Principles of Information Organization in Librarianship" by Vlalmir Slamecka and Mortimer Taube all published in Library Quarterly, vol. 34 (1964). "The United States Library of Congress Automation Survey" by B.E. Markuson in UNESCO Bulletin for Libraries, vol. 19 (January-February, 1965).

4 Markuson, B.E. "A System Development Study for the Library of Congress Automation Program" (Library Quarterly 36(2):197-233, July, 1966).

5 Library of Congress, Information Systems Office Project MARC, An Experiment in Automating Library of Congress Catalog Data (Washington D.C., Library of Congress, June, 1967).

6 Markuson, B.E. "A System Development Study for the Library of Congress Automation Program." op. cit.

Library of Congress
National Referral Center

The National Referral Center for Science and Technology was established in the Reference Department of the Library of Congress in 1963, aided by a grant from the National Science Foundation to put scientists and technologists looking for specialized information into direct contact with those who can provide it.

John F. Stearns, Chief, National Referral Center, described the Center as "... a clearinghouse to provide comprehensive, coordinated access to the nation's resources of scientific and technical information." The information resource has been interpreted as "any organization, facility, or individual willing and able to give authoritative responses to scientific or technical enquiries out of an existing store of knowledge or expertise." The functions of the Center are: (1) the identification of all significant information resources in the field of science and technology; (2) the acquisition, cataloging, and correlation of substantive and procedural data defining the nature, scope, and capabilities of these resources; (3) the provision of advice and guidance about these resources to any organization or individual requiring access to them by responding to requests for referral assistance and by publishing directories and guides in selected subject fields; and (4) the exploration, through actual operating experience, of the roles and relationships that exist or should exist among the many elements of the scientific and technical information complex.[1]

The Center does not, as a rule, attempt to answer the inquirer's questions directly but refers him to governmental or private organizations or to specialists who can provide the needed information. The requests for bibliographical information are referred to the pertinent division of the Library of Congress and other federal bodies engaged in the dissemination of scientific information.

As a clearinghouse the Center is actively engaged in compiling and updating an inventory of information resources covering different subjects. The inventory includes professional societies, institutes, research bureaus, federal and state government agencies, industrial laboratories, technical and special libraries, information and documentation centers, and abstracting and indexing services.

Besides maintaining the updated inventory of detailed data on special information resources for the Center's own use, a program is underway for the issuance of special directories of such resources in printed form. So far four volumes of the directories of information resources in the United States covering the physical, biological and engineering sciences (Volume 1); the social sciences (Volume 2); water, other than oceanography (Volume 3); and federal government (Volume 4) have been compiled and published. Each resource in the directory is described in terms of subject coverage, collections, services, and publications. These directories serve as useful reference tools in libraries and technical information centers to establish direct inter-communication where possible.

The referral service provided by the Center is continuously evaluated by a follow-up letter sent out approximately 90 days after answering the request in each case. A statistical analysis of the answers received reveals that 77 percent rated the referrals as useful, 15 percent rated them as equivocal, and only 8 percent rated them as of no help. More than 50 percent of the inquiries are from industry. Industrial establishments, particularly the smaller ones which do not have technical information facilities of their own, find the service very helpful.

Bibliographical References

1 Stearns, John F. "National Referral Center's First Year" (Special Libraries 55(1):20-23, January, 1964).

Massachusetts Institute of Technology
Technical Information Project (TIP)

Dr. M. M. Kessler has developed, as a part of the MAC Project, an interesting information storage and retrieval system at the MIT Library. This experimental design commonly known as TIP (Technical Information Project)[1] is aimed at evaluating search strategies and studying the role of human factors in literature search, besides investigating computer capabilities and cost analysis. Dr. Kessler described the model of the project in the following words:

> In its present configuration, a user may sit at an electric typewriter, scan a stated range of literature and perform a search based on key words, key word in context, citation index, bibliographic coupling, author, location and various combinations of these. The response is printed back on the same typewriter within seconds of the request. The inter-relation between the user and the system is free of intermediaries and is accomplished by means of language very close to natural English. [2]

The experiment is based on physics literature published in twenty-one core journals on the subject. The specific journals were chosen on the associative statistics of the various journals determined by the frequency of inter-journal references.

In his article "Some Statistical Properties of Citations in the Literature of Physics,"[3] Dr. Kessler has given a very clear explanation of the statistical techniques he used in determining the family matrix of the journals.

The bibliographic information (author, institutional affiliation of the author, title, location) of each article, the citations (journal, volume, page), the location of the article in Physics Abstracts, and the available subject index information, are all punched on cards and after verification transferred to magnetic tape for storage. The computer edited tape is then transferred to an assigned location on the computer disc memory for manipulation and search. Storage on the computer disc is growing at the rate of 1,500 items per month which is about 50 to 60 percent of all papers abstracted in Physics Abstract.

The computer configuration is the time-sharing central computer IBM 7090 and one hundred remote typewriter consoles. These consoles are distributed at various faculties and other locations around the MIT campus.

A set of programs has been developed under the general name SHARE and the set is available to all users at the remote consoles. By typing "RESUME FILE" the user may receive the updated list of journals and other titles in the computer disc memory. The user may also get the list of programs, with short descriptions, by instructing the typewriter console to print that.

The use of typewriter terminals linked to a central computer has no doubt enlarged the scope of computer use in information processing. The use of terminals circumvents the delay in delivering bibliographic information from the remote area to a main processing center.

Dr. Saunborn C. Brown's experiment[4] with the TIP service for updating the bibliographic data of his book on plasma physics is an interesting record of the efficiency of this experimental search system.

Bibliographical References

1 Kessler, M. M., Ivie, E. L. and Mathews, W. D. "The M. I. T. Technical Information Project: a prototype system" (Proceedings American Documentation Institute, vol. 1, 1964).

2 Kessler, M. M. "The MIT, Technical Information Project" (Physics To-day, March 1965, p. 28-36).

3 Kessler, M. M. "Some Statistical Properties of Citation in the Literature of Physics" To be published.

4 Brown, Saunborn C. "A Bibliographical Search by Computer" (Physics To-day, vol. 19, no. 5).

Massachusetts Institute of Technology
Project: INTREX

At the Massachusetts Institute of Technology a fundamental research program on information transfer systems named INTREX (Information Transfer Experiments)[1] has been started under the guidance of Dr. C. F. J. Overhage. Dr. Overhage and a group of his associates at the MIT School of Engineering are investigating, in collaboration with the MIT Libraries, long-term solutions for the operational problems of large libraries and development of on-line time-shared computer systems as a tool for more efficient direct communication between the user and the stored information in memory disc files.

The research and development activities of Project INTREX have been divided into four areas of work: an augmented catalog; full-text access; fact retrieval; and network integration. The overall objective is to design a new library service that might become operative at MIT and elsewhere by 1970.

Dr. Overhage describes the library of the future in the following way:

> In the university of the future as it is visualized at MIT, the library will be the central facility of an information-transfer network that will extend throughout the academic community. Students and scholars will use this network to gain access to the University's total information resources, through touch-tone telephones, teletypewriter key boards, television like displays, and quick made copies. The users of the system will communicate with each other as well as with the library; data just obtained in the laboratory and comments made by the observers will be easily available as text books in the library or documents in the departmental files.
>
> The information traffic will be controlled by means of the University's time-shared computer utility, much as today's verbal communications are handled by the campus telephone exchange. Long distance service will connect the University's information transfer network with sources and users elsewhere. [2]

The INTREX research team is now actively engaged in setting up a model library which will modernize current library procedures and in which experiments can be carried out on newer systems on information handling technology and on other new ideas.

In the area of augmented catalogs, a cataloging manual standardizing the catalog entries in machine-readable form and the design of the augmented-catalog storage and retrieval system have been completed. The research team is working on the experimental design of a computer-stored augmented catalog for materials in selected areas of science and technology and is exploring techniques that may ultimately lead to an ability to provide rapid access to full textual material at remote terminals.

A display console for an on-line computer system is also being designed and tested as a part of the augmented catalog program since the existing on-line computer terminals do not meet the requirements for the console to be used for user interaction with an augmented catalog. The semiannual activity report of the Project gives a clear idea of the console design and its capability:

> The efforts are directed towards designing a console which uses a cathode-ray-tube display with approximately 2,000 alphanumeric-character capacity. A data-communication rate between central computer and console groups of 200 characters per second is envisioned. Several character sets should be possible in addition to the English alphabet. User communications are entered by means of a typewriter key board, and special function buttons designate frequently encountered commands. The user's message is displayed on the cathode-ray-tube prior to the transmission to the time-shared computer, and editing of displayed commands is possible. As the user's conversation with the catalog system progresses, certain data supplied by the computer may be stored locally for future reference, edited as required, and eventually printed in hard copy form. [3]

Experiments are also being made to determine the speed capabilities, quality of output, and other operating characteristics of a display system which consists of a television display tube with a flying-spot-scanner.

In the area of full-text access, a comparative study is being made of various off-line storage media such as microform, magnetic media, and photo-optical devices to determine the suitability of these media when used in a library. Various optimum parameters for display equipment, such as the number of scan lines, brightness, contrast and techniques for obtaining low cost hard copy, are also under investigation. An experimental system has been designed to transmit microfilm images and to produce facsimile reproduction at the receiving stations. It is predicted that in the future the time required to gain access to a document or to information may be eliminated by generating microform or hard copies at a distance by signals transmitted over electrical circuits in either analog or digital form.

In the area of fact retrieval, an experiment is underway to develop systems for rapid processing of the data in large files to provide a computer-based data bank for retrieval and assembly of facts for automatic answering of the questions.

The INTREX program also plans to develop the network concept of information retrieval and for that purpose is working on an experimental design using the MEDLARS and NASA computer-aided literature search services.

Bibliographical References

1 Overhage, C. F. L., and Harman, R. J. INTREX, Report of a Planning Conference on Information Transfer Experiments. Cambridge, Mass., The M. I. T. Press, 1965.

2 Overhage, C. F. J. "Plans for Project INTREX" Science 152:1032-1037, May 20, 1966).

3 MIT. INTREX Project, semiannual activity report, (September 15, 1966 to March 15, 1967) p. 16.